I0455809

The Presidential Debates of 2016

Edited by Richard P. Hardwood, III

©2017 FREEDOM PRESS

Printed in the USA
Library of Congress Cataloging in Publication Data
ISBN-13: 978-1547153497
ISBN- 1547153490
Hardwood, Richard P, III

Editor's Note:

The Three Presidential Debates during 2016 laid the groundwork for the Presidential Election.

Below is the full transcript from the debates.

Rarely do we get to realize we are watching history "in the making." I Believe this series of events will mark the beginning of one of the most turbulent and amazing times in our 240+ year history. When it is over everything will have changed. This transcript is compiled to allow the 'everyday man' the chance to read it without interference.

Read it...   review it...   enjoy it!

Excelsior!!

Richard P Hardwood, III

Table of Contents

FIRST
PRESIDENTIAL
DEBATE

1 Hillary Clinton and Donald Trump went head-to-head for
2 the first time Monday night in a debate at Hofstra
3 University in Hempstead, N.Y. The debate was moderated
4 by Lester Holt of NBC News and came as polls both
5 nationally and in swing states are increasingly tight.
6
7 **LESTER HOLT:** Good evening from Hofstra University in
8 Hempstead, New York. I'm Lester Holt, anchor of "NBC
9 Nightly News." I want to welcome you to the first
10 presidential debate.
11
12 The participants tonight are Donald Trump and Hillary
13 Clinton. This debate is sponsored by the Commission on
14 Presidential   Debates,   a   nonpartisan,   nonprofit
15 organization. The commission drafted tonight's format,
16 and the rules have been agreed to by the campaigns.
17
18 The 90-minute debate is divided into six segments, each
19 15 minutes long. We'll explore three topic areas tonight:

1 Achieving prosperity; America's direction; and securing
2 America. At the start of each segment, I will ask the same
3 lead-off question to both candidates, and they will each
4 have up to two minutes to respond. From that point until
5 the end of the segment, we'll have an open discussion.
6
7 The questions are mine and have not been shared with the
8 commission or the campaigns. The audience here in the
9 room has agreed to remain silent so that we can focus on
10 what the candidates are saying.
11
12 I will invite you to applaud, however, at this moment, as
13 we welcome the candidates: Democratic nominee for
14 president of the United States, Hillary Clinton, and
15 Republican nominee for president of the United States,
16 Donald J. Trump.
17
18 **(APPLAUSE)**
19
20 **CLINTON:** How are you, Donald?
21
22 **(APPLAUSE)**
23
24 **HOLT:** Good luck to you.
25
26 **(APPLAUSE)**
27
28 Well, I don't expect us to cover all the issues of this
29 campaign tonight, but I remind everyone, there are two
30 more presidential debates scheduled. We are going to
31 focus on many of the issues that voters tell us are most
32 important, and we're going to press for specifics. I am
33 honored to have this role, but this evening belongs to the
34 candidates and, just as important, to the American people.

1
2 Candidates, we look forward to hearing you articulate your
3 policies and your positions, as well as your visions and
4 your values. So, let's begin.
5
6 We're calling this opening segment "Achieving Prosperity."
7 And central to that is jobs. There are two economic
8 realities in America today. There's been a record six
9 straight years of job growth, and new census numbers
10 show incomes have increased at a record rate after years
11 of stagnation. However, income inequality remains
12 significant, and nearly half of Americans are living
13 paycheck to paycheck.
14
15 Beginning with you, Secretary Clinton, why are you a
16 better choice than your opponent to create the kinds of
17 jobs that will put more money into the pockets of
18 American works?
19
20 **CLINTON:** Well, thank you, Lester, and thanks to Hofstra
21 for hosting us.
22
23 The central question in this election is really what kind of
24 country we want to be and what kind of future we'll build
25 together. Today is my granddaughter's second birthday, so
26 I think about this a lot. First, we have to build an economy
27 that works for everyone, not just those at the top. That
28 means we need new jobs, good jobs, with rising incomes.
29
30 I want us to invest in you. I want us to invest in your
31 future. That means jobs in infrastructure, in advanced
32 manufacturing, innovation and technology, clean,
33 renewable energy, and small business, because most of
34 the new jobs will come from small business. We also have

1 to make the economy fairer. That starts with raising the
2 national minimum wage and also guarantee, finally, equal
3 pay for women's work.
4
5 **CLINTON:** I also want to see more companies do profit-
6 sharing. If you help create the profits, you should be able
7 to share in them, not just the executives at the top.
8
9 And I want us to do more to support people who are
10 struggling to balance family and work. I've heard from so
11 many of you about the difficult choices you face and the
12 stresses that you're under. So let's have paid family leave,
13 earned sick days. Let's be sure we have affordable child
14 care and debt-free college.
15
16 How are we going to do it? We're going to do it by having
17 the wealthy pay their fair share and close the corporate
18 loopholes.
19
20 Finally, we tonight are on the stage together, Donald
21 Trump and I. Donald, it's good to be with you. We're going
22 to have a debate where we are talking about the
23 important issues facing our country. You have to judge us,
24 who can shoulder the immense, awesome responsibilities
25 of the presidency, who can put into action the plans that
26 will make your life better. I hope that I will be able to earn
27 your vote on November 8th.
28
29 **HOLT:** Secretary Clinton, thank you.
30
31 Mr. Trump, the same question to you. It's about putting
32 money -- more money into the pockets of American
33 workers. You have up to two minutes.
34

1   **TRUMP:** Thank you, Lester. Our jobs are fleeing the
2   country. They're going to Mexico. They're going to many
3   other countries. You look at what China is doing to our
4   country in terms of making our product. They're devaluing
5   their currency, and there's nobody in our government to
6   fight them. And we have a very good fight. And we have a
7   winning fight. Because they're using our country as a piggy
8   bank to rebuild China, and many other countries are doing
9   the same thing.
10
11   So we're losing our good jobs, so many of them. When you
12   look at what's happening in Mexico, a friend of mine who
13   builds plants said it's the eighth wonder of the world.
14   They're building some of the biggest plants anywhere in
15   the world, some of the most sophisticated, some of the
16   best plants. With the United States, as he said, not so
17   much.
18
19   So Ford is leaving. You see that, their small car division
20   leaving. Thousands of jobs leaving Michigan, leaving Ohio.
21   They're all leaving. And we can't allow it to happen
22   anymore. As far as child care is concerned and so many
23   other things, I think Hillary and I agree on that. We
24   probably disagree a little bit as to numbers and amounts
25   and what we're going to do, but perhaps we'll be talking
26   about that later.
27
28   But we have to stop our jobs from being stolen from us.
29   We have to stop our companies from leaving the United
30   States and, with it, firing all of their people. All you have to
31   do is take a look at Carrier air conditioning in Indianapolis.
32   They left -- fired 1,400 people. They're going to Mexico. So
33   many hundreds and hundreds of companies are doing this.
34

1   **TRUMP:** We cannot let it happen. Under my plan, I'll be
2   reducing taxes tremendously, from 35 percent to 15
3   percent for companies, small and big businesses. That's
4   going to be a job creator like we haven't seen since Ronald
5   Reagan. It's going to be a beautiful thing to watch.
6
7   Companies will come. They will build. They will expand.
8   New companies will start. And I look very, very much
9   forward to doing it. We have to renegotiate our trade
10 deals, and we have to stop these countries from stealing
11 our companies and our jobs.
12
13 **HOLT:** Secretary Clinton, would you like to respond?
14
15 **CLINTON:** Well, I think that trade is an important issue. Of
16 course, we are 5 percent of the world's population; we
17 have to trade with the other 95 percent. And we need to
18 have smart, fair trade deals.
19
20 We also, though, need to have a tax system that rewards
21 work and not just financial transactions. And the kind of
22 plan that Donald has put forth would be trickle-down
23 economics all over again. In fact, it would be the most
24 extreme version, the biggest tax cuts for the top percent
25 of the people in this country than we've ever had.
26
27 I call it trumped-up trickle-down, because that's exactly
28 what it would be. That is not how we grow the economy.
29
30 We just have a different view about what's best for
31 growing the economy, how we make investments that will
32 actually produce jobs and rising incomes.
33

1 I think we come at it from somewhat different
2 perspectives. I understand that. You know, Donald was
3 very fortunate in his life, and that's all to his benefit. He
4 started his business with $14 million, borrowed from his
5 father, and he really believes that the more you help
6 wealthy people, the better off we'll be and that everything
7 will work out from there.
8
9 I don't buy that. I have a different experience. My father
10 was a small-businessman. He worked really hard. He
11 printed drapery fabrics on long tables, where he pulled out
12 those fabrics and he went down with a silkscreen and
13 dumped the paint in and took the squeegee and kept
14 going.
15
16 And so what I believe is the more we can do for the middle
17 class, the more we can invest in you, your education, your
18 skills, your future, the better we will be off and the better
19 we'll grow. That's the kind of economy I want us to see
20 again.
21
22 **HOLT:** Let me follow up with Mr. Trump, if you can. You've
23 talked about creating 25 million jobs, and you've promised
24 to bring back millions of jobs for Americans. How are you
25 going to bring back the industries that have left this
26 country for cheaper labor overseas? How, specifically, are
27 you going to tell American manufacturers that you have to
28 come back?
29
30 **TRUMP:** Well, for one thing -- and before we start on that -
31 - my father gave me a very small loan in 1975, and I built it
32 into a company that's worth many, many billions of
33 dollars, with some of the greatest assets in the world, and

1 I say that only because that's the kind of thinking that our
2 country needs.
3
4 Our country's in deep trouble. We don't know what we're
5 doing when it comes to devaluations and all of these
6 countries all over the world, especially China. They're the
7 best, the best ever at it. What they're doing to us is a very,
8 very sad thing.
9
10 So we have to do that. We have to renegotiate our trade
11 deals. And, Lester, they're taking our jobs, they're giving
12 incentives, they're doing things that, frankly, we don't do.
13
14 Let me give you the example of Mexico. They have a VAT
15 tax. We're on a different system. When we sell into
16 Mexico, there's a tax. When they sell in -- automatic, 16
17 percent, approximately. When they sell into us, there's no
18 tax. It's a defective agreement. It's been defective for a
19 long time, many years, but the politicians haven't done
20 anything about it.
21
22 Now, in all fairness to Secretary Clinton -- yes, is that OK?
23 Good. I want you to be very happy. It's very important to
24 me.
25
26 But in all fairness to Secretary Clinton, when she started
27 talking about this, it was really very recently. She's been
28 doing this for 30 years. And why hasn't she made the
29 agreements better? The NAFTA agreement is defective.
30 Just because of the tax and many other reasons, but just
31 because of the fact...
32
33 **HOLT:** Let me interrupt just a moment, but...
34

1 **TRUMP:** Secretary Clinton and others, politicians, should
2 have been doing this for years, not right now, because of
3 the fact that we've created a movement. They should have
4 been doing this for years. What's happened to our jobs
5 and our country and our economy generally is -- look, we
6 owe $20 trillion. We cannot do it any longer, Lester. **HOLT:**
7 Back to the question, though. How do you bring back --
8 specifically bring back jobs, American manufacturers? How
9 do you make them bring the jobs back?
10
11 **TRUMP:** Well, the first thing you do is don't let the jobs
12 leave. The companies are leaving. I could name, I mean,
13 there are thousands of them. They're leaving, and they're
14 leaving in bigger numbers than ever.
15
16 And what you do is you say, fine, you want to go to Mexico
17 or some other country, good luck. We wish you a lot of
18 luck. But if you think you're going to make your air
19 conditioners or your cars or your cookies or whatever you
20 make and bring them into our country without a tax,
21 you're wrong.
22
23 And once you say you're going to have to tax them coming
24 in, and our politicians never do this, because they have
25 special interests and the special interests want those
26 companies to leave, because in many cases, they own the
27 companies. So what I'm saying is, we can stop them from
28 leaving. We have to stop them from leaving. And that's a
29 big, big factor.
30
31 **HOLT:** Let me let Secretary Clinton get in here.
32
33 **CLINTON:** Well, let's stop for a second and remember
34 where we were eight years ago. We had the worst

1 financial crisis, the Great Recession, the worst since the
2 1930s. That was in large part because of tax policies that
3 slashed taxes on the wealthy, failed to invest in the middle
4 class, took their eyes off of Wall Street, and created a
5 perfect storm.
6
7 In fact, Donald was one of the people who rooted for the
8 housing crisis. He said, back in 2006, "Gee, I hope it does
9 collapse, because then I can go in and buy some and make
10 some money." Well, it did collapse.
11
12 **TRUMP:** That's called business, by the way.
13
14 **CLINTON:** Nine million people -- nine million people lost
15 their jobs. Five million people lost their homes. And $13
16 trillion in family wealth was wiped out.
17
18 Now, we have come back from that abyss. And it has not
19 been easy. So we're now on the precipice of having a
20 potentially much better economy, but the last thing we
21 need to do is to go back to the policies that failed us in the
22 first place.
23
24 Independent experts have looked at what I've proposed
25 and looked at what Donald's proposed, and basically
26 they've said this, that if his tax plan, which would blow up
27 the debt by over $5 trillion and would in some instances
28 disadvantage middle-class families compared to the
29 wealthy, were to go into effect, we would lose 3.5 million
30 jobs and maybe have another recession.
31
32 They've looked at my plans and they've said, OK, if we can
33 do this, and I intend to get it done, we will have 10 million
34 more new jobs, because we will be making investments

1   where we can grow the economy. Take clean energy.
2   Some country is going to be the clean- energy superpower
3   of the 21st century. Donald thinks that climate change is a
4   hoax perpetrated by the Chinese. I think it's real.
5
6   **TRUMP:** I did not. I did not. I do not say that.
7
8   **CLINTON:** I think science is real.
9
10 **TRUMP:** I do not say that.
11
12 **CLINTON:** And I think it's important that we grip this and
13 deal with it, both at home and abroad. And here's what we
14 can do. We can deploy a half a billion more solar panels.
15 We can have enough clean energy to power every home.
16 We can build a new modern electric grid. That's a lot of
17 jobs; that's a lot of new economic activity.
18
19 So I've tried to be very specific about what we can and
20 should do, and I am determined that we're going to get
21 the economy really moving again, building on the progress
22 we've made over the last eight years, but never going back
23 to what got us in trouble in the first place.
24
25 **HOLT:** Mr. Trump?
26
27 **TRUMP:** She talks about solar panels. We invested in a
28 solar company, our country. That was a disaster. They lost
29 plenty of money on that one.
30
31 Now, look, I'm a great believer in all forms of energy, but
32 we're putting a lot of people out of work. Our energy
33 policies are a disaster. Our country is losing so much in

11

1 terms of energy, in terms of paying off our debt. You can't
2 do what you're looking to do with $20 trillion in debt.
3
4 The Obama administration, from the time they've come in,
5 is over 230 years' worth of debt, and he's topped it. He's
6 doubled it in a course of almost eight years, seven-and-a-
7 half years, to be semi- exact.
8
9 So I will tell you this. We have to do a much better job at
10 keeping our jobs. And we have to do a much better job at
11 giving companies incentives to build new companies or to
12 expand, because they're not doing it.
13
14 And all you have to do is look at Michigan and look at Ohio
15 and look at all of these places where so many of their jobs
16 and their companies are just leaving, they're gone.
17
18 And, Hillary, I'd just ask you this. You've been doing this for
19 30 years. Why are you just thinking about these solutions
20 right now? For 30 years, you've been doing it, and now
21 you're just starting to think of solutions.
22
23 **CLINTON:** Well, actually...
24
25 **TRUMP:** I will bring -- excuse me. I will bring back jobs. You
26 can't bring back jobs.
27
28 **CLINTON:** Well, actually, I have thought about this quite a
29 bit.
30
31 **TRUMP:** Yeah, for 30 years.
32

1 **CLINTON:** And I have -- well, not quite that long. I think my
2 husband did a pretty good job in the 1990s. I think a lot
3 about what worked and how we can make it work again...
4
5 **TRUMP:** Well, he approved NAFTA...
6
7   **(CROSSTALK)**
8
9 **CLINTON:** ... million new jobs, a balanced budget...
10
11 **TRUMP:** He approved NAFTA, which is the single worst
12 trade deal ever approved in this country.
13
14 **CLINTON:** Incomes went up for everybody. Manufacturing
15 jobs went up also in the 1990s, if we're actually going to
16 look at the facts.
17
18 When I was in the Senate, I had a number of trade deals
19 that came before me, and I held them all to the same test.
20 Will they create jobs in America? Will they raise incomes in
21 America? And are they good for our national security?
22 Some of them I voted for. The biggest one, a multinational
23 one known as CAFTA, I voted against. And because I hold
24 the same standards as I look at all of these trade deals.
25
26 But let's not assume that trade is the only challenge we
27 have in the economy. I think it is a part of it, and I've said
28 what I'm going to do. I'm going to have a special
29 prosecutor. We're going to enforce the trade deals we
30 have, and we're going to hold people accountable.
31
32 When I was secretary of state, we actually increased
33 American exports globally 30 percent. We increased them
34 to China 50 percent. So I know how to really work to get

13

1　new jobs and to get exports that helped to create more
2　new jobs.
3
4　**HOLT:** Very quickly...
5
6　**TRUMP:** But you haven't done it in 30 years or 26 years or
7　any number you want to...
8
9　**CLINTON:** Well, I've been a senator, Donald...
10
11　**TRUMP:** You haven't done it. You haven't done it.
12
13　**CLINTON:** And I have been a secretary of state...
14
15　**TRUMP:** Excuse me.
16
17　**CLINTON:** And I have done a lot...
18
19　**TRUMP:** Your husband signed NAFTA, which was one of
20　the worst things that ever happened to the manufacturing
21　industry.
22
23　**CLINTON:** Well, that's your opinion. That is your opinion.
24
25　**TRUMP:** You go to New England, you go to Ohio,
26　Pennsylvania, you go anywhere you want, Secretary
27　Clinton, and you will see devastation where manufacture
28　is down 30, 40, sometimes 50 percent. NAFTA is the worst
29　trade deal maybe ever signed anywhere, but certainly ever
30　signed in this country.
31
32　And now you want to approve Trans-Pacific Partnership.
33　You were totally in favor of it. Then you heard what I was
34　saying, how bad it is, and you said, I can't win that debate.

1 But you know that if you did win, you would approve that,
2 and that will be almost as bad as NAFTA. Nothing will ever
3 top NAFTA.
4
5 **CLINTON:** Well, that is just not accurate. I was against it
6 once it was finally negotiated and the terms were laid out.
7 I wrote about that in...
8
9 **TRUMP:** You called it the gold standard.
10
11   **(CROSSTALK)**
12
13 **TRUMP:** You called it the gold standard of trade deals. You
14 said it's the finest deal you've ever seen.
15
16 **CLINTON:** No.
17
18 **TRUMP:** And then you heard what I said about it, and all of
19 a sudden you were against it.
20
21 **CLINTON:** Well, Donald, I know you live in your own
22 reality, but that is not the facts. The facts are -- I did say I
23 hoped it would be a good deal, but when it was
24 negotiated...
25
26 **TRUMP:** Not.
27
28 **CLINTON:** ... which I was not responsible for, I concluded it
29 wasn't. I wrote about that in my book...
30
31 **TRUMP:** So is it President Obama's fault?
32
33 **CLINTON:** ... before you even announced.
34

1 **TRUMP:** Is it President Obama's fault?

2

3 **CLINTON:** Look, there are differences...

4

5 **TRUMP:** Secretary, is it President Obama's fault?

6

7 **CLINTON:** There are...

8

9 **TRUMP:** Because he's pushing it.

10

11 **CLINTON:** There are different views about what's good for
12 our country, our economy, and our leadership in the
13 world. And I think it's important to look at what we need
14 to do to get the economy going again. That's why I said
15 new jobs with rising incomes, investments, not in more tax
16 cuts that would add $5 trillion to the debt.

17

18 **TRUMP:** But you have no plan.

19

20 **CLINTON:** But in -- oh, but I do.

21

22 **TRUMP:** Secretary, you have no plan.

23

24 **CLINTON:** In fact, I have written a book about it. It's called
25 "Stronger Together." You can pick it up tomorrow at a
26 bookstore...

27

28 **TRUMP:** That's about all you've...

29

30 **(CROSSTALK)**

31

32 **HOLT:** Folks, we're going to...

33

34 **CLINTON:** ... or at an airport near you.

1
2 **HOLT:** We're going to move to...
3
4 **CLINTON:** But it's because I see this -- we need to have
5 strong growth, fair growth, sustained growth. We also
6 have to look at how we help families balance the
7 responsibilities at home and the responsibilities at
8 business.
9
10 So we have a very robust set of plans. And people have
11 looked at both of our plans, have concluded that mine
12 would create 10 million jobs and yours would lose us 3.5
13 million jobs, and explode the debt which would have a
14 recession.
15
16 **TRUMP:** You are going to approve one of the biggest tax
17 cuts in history. You are going to approve one of the biggest
18 tax increases in history. You are going to drive business
19 out. Your regulations are a disaster, and you're going to
20 increase regulations all over the place.
21
22 And by the way, my tax cut is the biggest since Ronald
23 Reagan. I'm very proud of it. It will create tremendous
24 numbers of new jobs. But regulations, you are going to
25 regulate these businesses out of existence.
26
27 When I go around -- Lester, I tell you this, I've been all
28 over. And when I go around, despite the tax cut, the thing
29 -- the things that business as in people like the most is the
30 fact that I'm cutting regulation. You have regulations on
31 top of regulations, and new companies cannot form and
32 old companies are going out of business. And you want to
33 increase the regulations and make them even worse.
34

1 I'm going to cut regulations. I'm going to cut taxes big
2 league, and you're going to raise taxes big league, end of
3 story.
4
5 **HOLT:** Let me get you to pause right there, because we're
6 going to move into -- we're going to move into the next
7 segment. We're going to talk taxes...
8
9 **CLINTON:** That can't -- that can't be left to stand.
10
11 **HOLT:** Please just take 30 seconds and then we're going to
12 go on.
13
14 **CLINTON:** I kind of assumed that there would be a lot of
15 these charges and claims, and so...
16
17 **TRUMP:** Facts.
18
19 **CLINTON:** So we have taken the home page of my website,
20 HillaryClinton.com, and we've turned it into a fact-checker.
21 So if you want to see in real-time what the facts are,
22 please go and take a look. Because what I have proposed...
23
24 **TRUMP:** And take a look at mine, also, and you'll see.
25
26 **CLINTON:** ... would not add a penny to the debt, and your
27 plans would add $5 trillion to the debt. What I have
28 proposed would cut regulations and streamline them for
29 small businesses. What I have proposed would be paid for
30 by raising taxes on the wealthy, because they have made
31 all the gains in the economy. And I think it's time that the
32 wealthy and corporations paid their fair share to support
33 this country.
34

1 **HOLT:** Well, you just opened the next segment.
2
3 **TRUMP:** Well, could I just finish -- I think I...
4
5 **(CROSSTALK)**
6
7 **HOLT:** I'm going to give you a chance right here...
8
9 **TRUMP:** I think I should -- you go to her website, and you
10 take a look at her website.
11
12 **HOLT:** ... with a new 15-minute segment...
13
14 **TRUMP:** She's going to raise taxes $1.3 trillion.
15
16 **HOLT:** Mr. Trump, I'm going to...
17
18 **TRUMP:** And look at her website. You know what? It's no
19 difference than this. She's telling us how to fight ISIS. Just
20 go to her website. She tells you how to fight ISIS on her
21 website. I don't think General Douglas MacArthur would
22 like that too much.
23
24 **HOLT:** The next segment, we're continuing...
25
26 **CLINTON:** Well, at least I have a plan to fight ISIS.
27
28 **HOLT:** ... achieving prosperity...
29
30 **TRUMP:** No, no, you're telling the enemy everything you
31 want to do.
32
33 **CLINTON:** No, we're not. No, we're not.
34

1   **TRUMP:** See, you're telling the enemy everything you
2   want to do. No wonder you've been fighting -- no wonder
3   you've been fighting ISIS your entire adult life.
4
5   **CLINTON:** That's a -- that's -- go to the -- please, fact
6   checkers, get to work.
7
8   **HOLT:** OK, you are unpacking a lot here. And we're still on
9   the issue of achieving prosperity. And I want to talk about
10 taxes. The fundamental difference between the two of you
11 concerns the wealthy.
12
13 Secretary Clinton, you're calling for a tax increase on the
14 wealthiest Americans. I'd like you to further defend that.
15 And, Mr. Trump, you're calling for tax cuts for the wealthy.
16 I'd like you to defend that. And this next two-minute
17 answer goes to you, Mr. Trump.
18
19 **TRUMP:** Well, I'm really calling for major jobs, because the
20 wealthy are going create tremendous jobs. They're going
21 to expand their companies. They're going to do a
22 tremendous job.
23
24 I'm getting rid of the carried interest provision. And if you
25 really look, it's not a tax -- it's really not a great thing for
26 the wealthy. It's a great thing for the middle class. It's a
27 great thing for companies to expand.
28
29 And when these people are going to put billions and
30 billions of dollars into companies, and when they're going
31 to bring $2.5 trillion back from overseas, where they can't
32 bring the money back, because politicians like Secretary
33 Clinton won't allow them to bring the money back,

1 because the taxes are so onerous, and the bureaucratic
2 red tape, so what -- is so bad.
3
4 So what they're doing is they're leaving our country, and
5 they're, believe it or not, leaving because taxes are too
6 high and because some of them have lots of money
7 outside of our country. And instead of bringing it back and
8 putting the money to work, because they can't work out a
9 deal to -- and everybody agrees it should be brought back.
10
11 Instead of that, they're leaving our country to get their
12 money, because they can't bring their money back into our
13 country, because of bureaucratic red tape, because they
14 can't get together. Because we have -- we have a president
15 that can't sit them around a table and get them to approve
16 something.
17
18 And here's the thing. Republicans and Democrats agree
19 that this should be done, $2.5 trillion. I happen to think it's
20 double that. It's probably $5 trillion that we can't bring
21 into our country, Lester. And with a little leadership, you'd
22 get it in here very quickly, and it could be put to use on the
23 inner cities and lots of other things, and it would be
24 beautiful.
25
26 But we have no leadership. And honestly, that starts with
27 Secretary Clinton.
28
29 **HOLT:** All right. You have two minutes of the same
30 question to defend tax increases on the wealthiest
31 Americans, Secretary Clinton.
32

1 **CLINTON:** I have a feeling that by, the end of this evening,
2 I'm going to be blamed for everything that's ever
3 happened.
4
5 **TRUMP:** Why not?
6
7 **CLINTON:** Why not? Yeah, why not?
8
9   **(LAUGHTER)**
10
11 You know, just join the debate by saying more crazy
12 things. Now, let me say this, it is absolutely the case...
13
14 **TRUMP:** There's nothing crazy about not letting our
15 companies bring their money back into their country.
16
17 **HOLT:** This is -- this is Secretary Clinton's two minutes,
18 please.
19
20 **TRUMP:** Yes.
21
22 **CLINTON:** Yeah, well, let's start the clock again, Lester.
23 We've looked at your tax proposals. I don't see changes in
24 the corporate tax rates or the kinds of proposals you're
25 referring to that would cause the repatriation, bringing
26 back of money that's stranded overseas. I happen to
27 support that.
28
29 **TRUMP:** Then you didn't read it.
30
31 **CLINTON:** I happen to -- I happen to support that in a way
32 that will actually work to our benefit. But when I look at
33 what you have proposed, you have what is called now the
34 Trump loophole, because it would so advantage you and

1 the business you do. You've proposed an approach that
2 has a...
3
4 **TRUMP:** Who gave it that name? The first I've -- who gave
5 it that name?
6
7 **(CROSSTALK)**
8
9 **HOLT:** Mr. Trump, this is Secretary Clinton's two minutes.
10
11 **CLINTON:** ... $4 billion tax benefit for your family. And
12 when you look at what you are proposing...
13
14 **TRUMP:** How much? How much for my family?
15
16 **CLINTON:** ... it is...
17
18 **TRUMP:** Lester, how much?
19
20 **CLINTON:** ... as I said, trumped-up trickle-down. Trickle-
21 down did not work. It got us into the mess we were in, in
22 2008 and 2009. Slashing taxes on the wealthy hasn't
23 worked.
24
25 And a lot of really smart, wealthy people know that. And
26 they are saying, hey, we need to do more to make the
27 contributions we should be making to rebuild the middle
28 class.
29
30 **CLINTON:** I don't think top-down works in America. I think
31 building the middle class, investing in the middle class,
32 making college debt-free so more young people can get
33 their education, helping people refinance their -- their
34 debt from college at a lower rate. Those are the kinds of

1 things that will really boost the economy. Broad-based,
2 inclusive growth is what we need in America, not more
3 advantages for people at the very top.
4
5 **HOLT:** Mr. Trump, we're...
6
7 **TRUMP:** Typical politician. All talk, no action. Sounds good,
8 doesn't work. Never going to happen. Our country is
9 suffering because people like Secretary Clinton have made
10 such bad decisions in terms of our jobs and in terms of
11 what's going on.
12
13 Now, look, we have the worst revival of an economy since
14 the Great Depression. And believe me: We're in a bubble
15 right now. And the only thing that looks good is the stock
16 market, but if you raise interest rates even a little bit,
17 that's going to come crashing down.
18
19 We are in a big, fat, ugly bubble. And we better be awfully
20 careful. And we have a Fed that's doing political things.
21 This Janet Yellen of the Fed. The Fed is doing political -- by
22 keeping the interest rates at this level. And believe me:
23 The day Obama goes off, and he leaves, and goes out to
24 the golf course for the rest of his life to play golf, when
25 they raise interest rates, you're going to see some very
26 bad things happen, because the Fed is not doing their job.
27 The Fed is being more political than Secretary Clinton.
28
29 **HOLT:** Mr. Trump, we're talking about the burden that
30 Americans have to pay, yet you have not released your tax
31 returns. And the reason nominees have released their
32 returns for decades is so that voters will know if their
33 potential president owes money to -- who he owes it to

1 and any business conflicts. Don't Americans have a right to
2 know if there are any conflicts of interest?
3
4 **TRUMP:** I don't mind releasing -- I'm under a routine audit.
5 And it'll be released. And -- as soon as the audit's finished,
6 it will be released.
7
8 But you will learn more about Donald Trump by going
9 down to the federal elections, where I filed a 104-page
10 essentially financial statement of sorts, the forms that they
11 have. It shows income -- in fact, the income -- I just looked
12 today -- the income is filed at $694 million for this past
13 year, $694 million. If you would have told me I was going
14 to make that 15 or 20 years ago, I would have been very
15 surprised.
16
17 But that's the kind of thinking that our country needs.
18 When we have a country that's doing so badly, that's being
19 ripped off by every single country in the world, it's the kind
20 of thinking that our country needs, because everybody --
21 Lester, we have a trade deficit with all of the countries
22 that we do business with, of almost $800 billion a year.
23 You know what that is? That means, who's negotiating
24 these trade deals?
25
26 We have people that are political hacks negotiating our
27 trade deals.
28
29 **HOLT:** The IRS says an audit...
30
31 **TRUMP:** Excuse me.
32

1 **HOLT:** ... of your taxes -- you're perfectly free to release
2 your taxes during an audit. And so the question, does the
3 public's right to know outweigh your personal...
4
5 **TRUMP:** Well, I told you, I will release them as soon as the
6 audit. Look, I've been under audit almost for 15 years. I
7 know a lot of wealthy people that have never been
8 audited. I said, do you get audited? I get audited almost
9 every year.
10
11 And in a way, I should be complaining. I'm not even
12 complaining. I don't mind it. It's almost become a way of
13 life. I get audited by the IRS. But other people don't.
14
15 I will say this. We have a situation in this country that has
16 to be taken care of. I will release my tax returns -- against
17 my lawyer's wishes -- when she releases her 33,000 e-
18 mails that have been deleted. As soon as she releases
19 them, I will release.
20
21 **(APPLAUSE)**
22
23 I will release my tax returns. And that's against -- my
24 lawyers, they say, "Don't do it." I will tell you this. No -- in
25 fact, watching shows, they're reading the papers. Almost
26 every lawyer says, you don't release your returns until the
27 audit's complete. When the audit's complete, I'll do it. But
28 I would go against them if she releases her e-mails.
29
30 **HOLT:** So it's negotiable?
31
32 **TRUMP:** It's not negotiable, no. Let her release the e-mails.
33 Why did she delete 33,000...
34

1 **HOLT:** Well, I'll let her answer that. But let me just
2 admonish the audience one more time. There was an
3 agreement. We did ask you to be silent, so it would be
4 helpful for us. Secretary Clinton?
5
6 **CLINTON:** Well, I think you've seen another example of
7 bait-and- switch here. For 40 years, everyone running for
8 president has released their tax returns. You can go and
9 see nearly, I think, 39, 40 years of our tax returns, but
10 everyone has done it. We know the IRS has made clear
11 there is no prohibition on releasing it when you're under
12 audit.
13
14 So you've got to ask yourself, why won't he release his tax
15 returns? And I think there may be a couple of reasons.
16 First, maybe he's not as rich as he says he is. Second,
17 maybe he's not as charitable as he claims to be.
18
19 **CLINTON:** Third, we don't know all of his business dealings,
20 but we have been told through investigative reporting that
21 he owes about $650 million to Wall Street and foreign
22 banks. Or maybe he doesn't want the American people, all
23 of you watching tonight, to know that he's paid nothing in
24 federal taxes, because the only years that anybody's ever
25 seen were a couple of years when he had to turn them
26 over to state authorities when he was trying to get a
27 casino license, and they showed he didn't pay any federal
28 income tax.
29
30 **TRUMP:** That makes me smart.
31
32 **CLINTON:** So if he's paid zero, that means zero for troops,
33 zero for vets, zero for schools or health. And I think
34 probably he's not all that enthusiastic about having the

27

1 rest of our country see what the real reasons are, because
2 it must be something really important, even terrible, that
3 he's trying to hide.
4
5 And the financial disclosure statements, they don't give
6 you the tax rate. They don't give you all the details that tax
7 returns would. And it just seems to me that this is
8 something that the American people deserve to see. And I
9 have no reason to believe that he's ever going to release
10 his tax returns, because there's something he's hiding.
11
12 And we'll guess. We'll keep guessing at what it might be
13 that he's hiding. But I think the question is, were he ever
14 to get near the White House, what would be those
15 conflicts? Who does he owe money to? Well, he owes you
16 the answers to that, and he should provide them.
17
18 **HOLT:** He also -- he also raised the issue of your e-mails.
19 Do you want to respond to that?
20
21 **CLINTON:** I do. You know, I made a mistake using a private
22 e- mail.
23
24 **TRUMP:** That's for sure.
25
26 **CLINTON:** And if I had to do it over again, I would,
27 obviously, do it differently. But I'm not going to make any
28 excuses. It was a mistake, and I take responsibility for that.
29
30 **HOLT:** Mr. Trump?
31
32 **TRUMP:** That was more than a mistake. That was done
33 purposely. OK? That was not a mistake. That was done
34 purposely. When you have your staff taking the Fifth

1 Amendment, taking the Fifth so they're not prosecuted,
2 when you have the man that set up the illegal server
3 taking the Fifth, I think it's disgraceful. And believe me, this
4 country thinks it's -- really thinks it's disgraceful, also.
5
6 As far as my tax returns, you don't learn that much from
7 tax returns. That I can tell you. You learn a lot from
8 financial disclosure. And you should go down and take a
9 look at that.
10
11 The other thing, I'm extremely underleveraged. The report
12 that said $650 -- which, by the way, a lot of friends of mine
13 that know my business say, boy, that's really not a lot of
14 money. It's not a lot of money relative to what I had.
15
16 The buildings that were in question, they said in the same
17 report, which was -- actually, it wasn't even a bad story, to
18 be honest with you, but the buildings are worth $3.9
19 billion. And the $650 isn't even on that. But it's not $650.
20 It's much less than that.
21
22 But I could give you a list of banks, I would -- if that would
23 help you, I would give you a list of banks. These are very
24 fine institutions, very fine banks. I could do that very
25 quickly.
26
27 I am very underleveraged. I have a great company. I have a
28 tremendous income. And the reason I say that is not in a
29 braggadocios way. It's because it's about time that this
30 country had somebody running it that has an idea about
31 money.
32
33 When we have $20 trillion in debt, and our country's a
34 mess, you know, it's one thing to have $20 trillion in debt

1 and our roads are good and our bridges are good and
2 everything's in great shape, our airports. Our airports are
3 like from a third world country.
4
5 You land at LaGuardia, you land at Kennedy, you land at
6 LAX, you land at Newark, and you come in from Dubai and
7 Qatar and you see these incredible -- you come in from
8 China, you see these incredible airports, and you land --
9 we've become a third world country.
10
11 So the worst of all things has happened. We owe $20
12 trillion, and we're a mess. We haven't even started. And
13 we've spent $6 trillion in the Middle East, according to a
14 report that I just saw. Whether it's 6 or 5, but it looks like
15 it's 6, $6 trillion in the Middle East, we could have rebuilt
16 our country twice.
17
18 And it's really a shame. And it's politicians like Secretary
19 Clinton that have caused this problem. Our country has
20 tremendous problems. We're a debtor nation. We're a
21 serious debtor nation. And we have a country that needs
22 new roads, new tunnels, new bridges, new airports, new
23 schools, new hospitals. And we don't have the money,
24 because it's been squandered on so many of your ideas.
25
26 **HOLT:** We'll let you respond and we'll move on to the next
27 segment.
28
29 **CLINTON:** And maybe because you haven't paid any
30 federal income tax for a lot of years.
31
32   **(APPLAUSE)**
33
34 And the other thing I think is important...

1
2 **TRUMP:** It would be squandered, too, believe me.
3
4 **CLINTON:** ... is if your -- if your main claim to be president
5 of the United States is your business, then I think we
6 should talk about that. You know, your campaign manager
7 said that you built a lot of businesses on the backs of little
8 guys.
9
10 And, indeed, I have met a lot of the people who were
11 stiffed by you and your businesses, Donald. I've met
12 dishwashers, painters, architects, glass installers, marble
13 installers, drapery installers, like my dad was, who you
14 refused to pay when they finished the work that you asked
15 them to do.
16
17 We have an architect in the audience who designed one of
18 your clubhouses at one of your golf courses. It's a beautiful
19 facility. It immediately was put to use. And you wouldn't
20 pay what the man needed to be paid, what he was
21 charging you to do...
22
23 **TRUMP:** Maybe he didn't do a good job and I was
24 unsatisfied with his work...
25
26 **CLINTON:** Well, to...
27
28 **TRUMP:** Which our country should do, too.
29
30 **CLINTON:** Do the thousands of people that you have
31 stiffed over the course of your business not deserve some
32 kind of apology from someone who has taken their labor,
33 taken the goods that they produced, and then refused to
34 pay them?

1
2 I can only say that I'm certainly relieved that my late father
3 never did business with you. He provided a good middle-
4 class life for us, but the people he worked for, he expected
5 the bargain to be kept on both sides.
6
7 And when we talk about your business, you've taken
8 business bankruptcy six times. There are a lot of great
9 businesspeople that have never taken bankruptcy once.
10 You call yourself the King of Debt. You talk about leverage.
11 You even at one time suggested that you would try to
12 negotiate down the national debt of the United States.
13
14 **TRUMP:** Wrong. Wrong.
15
16 **CLINTON:** Well, sometimes there's not a direct transfer of
17 skills from business to government, but sometimes what
18 happened in business would be really bad for government.
19
20 **HOLT:** Let's let Mr. Trump...
21
22 **CLINTON:** And we need to be very clear about that.
23
24 **TRUMP:** So, yeah, I think -- I do think it's time. Look, it's all
25 words, it's all sound bites. I built an unbelievable company.
26 Some of the greatest assets anywhere in the world, real
27 estate assets anywhere in the world, beyond the United
28 States, in Europe, lots of different places. It's an
29 unbelievable company.
30
31 But on occasion, four times, we used certain laws that are
32 there. And when Secretary Clinton talks about people that
33 didn't get paid, first of all, they did get paid a lot, but taken
34 advantage of the laws of the nation.

1
2 Now, if you want to change the laws, you've been there a
3 long time, change the laws. But I take advantage of the
4 laws of the nation because I'm running a company. My
5 obligation right now is to do well for myself, my family, my
6 employees, for my companies. And that's what I do.
7
8 But what she doesn't say is that tens of thousands of
9 people that are unbelievably happy and that love me. I'll
10 give you an example. We're just opening up on
11 Pennsylvania Avenue right next to the White House, so if I
12 don't get there one way, I'm going to get to Pennsylvania
13 Avenue another.
14
15 But we're opening the Old Post Office. Under budget,
16 ahead of schedule, saved tremendous money. I'm a year
17 ahead of schedule. And that's what this country should be
18 doing.
19
20 We build roads and they cost two and three and four times
21 what they're supposed to cost. We buy products for our
22 military and they come in at costs that are so far above
23 what they were supposed to be, because we don't have
24 people that know what they're doing.
25
26 When we look at the budget, the budget is bad to a large
27 extent because we have people that have no idea as to
28 what to do and how to buy. The Trump International is
29 way under budget and way ahead of schedule. And we
30 should be able to do that for our country.
31
32 **HOLT:** Well, we're well behind schedule, so I want to move
33 to our next segment. We move into our next segment

1 talking about America's direction. And let's start by talking
2 about race.
3
4 The share of Americans who say race relations are bad in
5 this country is the highest it's been in decades, much of it
6 amplified by shootings of African-Americans by police, as
7 we've seen recently in Charlotte and Tulsa. Race has been
8 a big issue in this campaign, and one of you is going to
9 have to bridge a very wide and bitter gap.
10
11 So how do you heal the divide? Secretary Clinton, you get
12 two minutes on this.
13
14 **CLINTON:** Well, you're right. Race remains a significant
15 challenge in our country. Unfortunately, race still
16 determines too much, often determines where people
17 live, determines what kind of education in their public
18 schools they can get, and, yes, it determines how they're
19 treated in the criminal justice system. We've just seen
20 those two tragic examples in both Tulsa and Charlotte.
21
22 And we've got to do several things at the same time. We
23 have to restore trust between communities and the police.
24 We have to work to make sure that our police are using
25 the best training, the best techniques, that they're well
26 prepared to use force only when necessary. Everyone
27 should be respected by the law, and everyone should
28 respect the law.
29
30 **CLINTON:** Right now, that's not the case in a lot of our
31 neighborhoods. So I have, ever since the first day of my
32 campaign, called for criminal justice reform. I've laid out a
33 platform that I think would begin to remedy some of the
34 problems we have in the criminal justice system.

1
2 But we also have to recognize, in addition to the
3 challenges that we face with policing, there are so many
4 good, brave police officers who equally want reform. So
5 we have to bring communities together in order to begin
6 working on that as a mutual goal. And we've got to get
7 guns out of the hands of people who should not have
8 them.
9
10 The gun epidemic is the leading cause of death of young
11 African- American men, more than the next nine causes
12 put together. So we have to do two things, as I said. We
13 have to restore trust. We have to work with the police. We
14 have to make sure they respect the communities and the
15 communities respect them. And we have to tackle the
16 plague of gun violence, which is a big contributor to a lot
17 of the problems that we're seeing today.
18
19 **HOLT:** All right, Mr. Trump, you have two minutes. How do
20 you heal the divide?
21
22 **TRUMP:** Well, first of all, Secretary Clinton doesn't want to
23 use a couple of words, and that's law and order. And we
24 need law and order. If we don't have it, we're not going to
25 have a country.
26
27 And when I look at what's going on in Charlotte, a city I
28 love, a city where I have investments, when I look at
29 what's going on throughout various parts of our country,
30 whether it's -- I mean, I can just keep naming them all day
31 long -- we need law and order in our country.
32
33 I just got today the, as you know, the endorsement of the
34 Fraternal Order of Police, we just -- just came in. We have

1 endorsements from, I think, almost every police group,
2 very -- I mean, a large percentage of them in the United
3 States.
4
5 We have a situation where we have our inner cities,
6 African- Americans, Hispanics are living in he'll because it's
7 so dangerous. You walk down the street, you get shot.
8
9 In Chicago, they've had thousands of shootings, thousands
10 since January 1st. Thousands of shootings. And I'm saying,
11 where is this? Is this a war-torn country? What are we
12 doing? And we have to stop the violence. We have to bring
13 back law and order. In a place like Chicago, where
14 thousands of people have been killed, thousands over the
15 last number of years, in fact, almost 4,000 have been killed
16 since Barack Obama became president, over -- almost
17 4,000 people in Chicago have been killed. We have to
18 bring back law and order.
19
20 Now, whether or not in a place like Chicago you do stop
21 and frisk, which worked very well, Mayor Giuliani is here,
22 worked very well in New York. It brought the crime rate
23 way down. But you take the gun away from criminals that
24 shouldn't be having it.
25
26 We have gangs roaming the street. And in many cases,
27 they're illegally here, illegal immigrants. And they have
28 guns. And they shoot people. And we have to be very
29 strong. And we have to be very vigilant.
30
31 We have to be -- we have to know what we're doing. Right
32 now, our police, in many cases, are afraid to do anything.
33 We have to protect our inner cities, because African-

1 American communities are being decimated by crime,
2 decimated.
3
4 **HOLT:** Your two -- your two minutes expired, but I do want
5 to follow up. Stop-and-frisk was ruled unconstitutional in
6 New York, because it largely singled out black and Hispanic
7 young men.
8
9 **TRUMP:** No, you're wrong. It went before a judge, who
10 was a very against-police judge. It was taken away from
11 her. And our mayor, our new mayor, refused to go forward
12 with the case. They would have won an appeal. If you look
13 at it, throughout the country, there are many places where
14 it's allowed.
15
16 **HOLT:** The argument is that it's a form of racial profiling.
17
18 **TRUMP:** No, the argument is that we have to take the
19 guns away from these people that have them and they are
20 bad people that shouldn't have them.
21
22 These are felons. These are people that are bad people
23 that shouldn't be -- when you have 3,000 shootings in
24 Chicago from January 1st, when you have 4,000 people
25 killed in Chicago by guns, from the beginning of the
26 presidency of Barack Obama, his hometown, you have to
27 have stop-and-frisk.
28
29 You need more police. You need a better community, you
30 know, relation. You don't have good community relations
31 in Chicago. It's terrible. I have property there. It's terrible
32 what's going on in Chicago.
33

1 But when you look -- and Chicago's not the only -- you go
2 to Ferguson, you go to so many different places. You need
3 better relationships. I agree with Secretary Clinton on this.
4
5 **TRUMP:** You need better relationships between the
6 communities and the police, because in some cases, it's
7 not good.
8
9 But you look at Dallas, where the relationships were really
10 studied, the relationships were really a beautiful thing, and
11 then five police officers were killed one night very
12 violently. So there's some bad things going on. Some really
13 bad things.
14
15 **HOLT:** Secretary Clinton...
16
17 **TRUMP:** But we need -- Lester, we need law and order.
18 And we need law and order in the inner cities, because the
19 people that are most affected by what's happening are
20 African-American and Hispanic people. And it's very unfair
21 to them what our politicians are allowing to happen.
22
23 **HOLT:** Secretary Clinton?
24
25 **CLINTON:** Well, I've heard -- I've heard Donald say this at
26 his rallies, and it's really unfortunate that he paints such a
27 dire negative picture of black communities in our country.
28
29 **TRUMP:** Ugh.
30
31 **CLINTON:** You know, the vibrancy of the black church, the
32 black businesses that employ so many people, the
33 opportunities that so many families are working to provide

1   for their kids. There's a lot that we should be proud of and
2   we should be supporting and lifting up.
3
4   But we do always have to make sure we keep people safe.
5   There are the right ways of doing it, and then there are
6   ways that are ineffective. Stop-and-frisk was found to be
7   unconstitutional and, in part, because it was ineffective. It
8   did not do what it needed to do.
9
10 Now, I believe in community policing. And, in fact, violent
11 crime is one-half of what it was in 1991. Property crime is
12 down 40 percent. We just don't want to see it creep back
13 up. We've had 25 years of very good cooperation.
14
15 But there were some problems, some unintended
16 consequences. Too many young African-American and
17 Latino men ended up in jail for nonviolent offenses. And
18 it's just a fact that if you're a young African-American man
19 and you do the same thing as a young white man, you are
20 more likely to be arrested, charged, convicted, and
21 incarcerated. So we've got to address the systemic racism
22 in our criminal justice system. We cannot just say law and
23 order. We have to say -- we have to come forward with a
24 plan that is going to divert people from the criminal justice
25 system, deal with mandatory minimum sentences, which
26 have put too many people away for too long for doing too
27 little.
28
29 We need to have more second chance programs. I'm glad
30 that we're ending private prisons in the federal system; I
31 want to see them ended in the state system. You shouldn't
32 have a profit motivation to fill prison cells with young
33 Americans. So there are some positive ways we can work
34 on this.

1

2 And I believe strongly that commonsense gun safety
3 measures would assist us. Right now -- and this is
4 something Donald has supported, along with the gun
5 lobby -- right now, we've got too many military- style
6 weapons on the streets. In a lot of places, our police are
7 outgunned. We need comprehensive background checks,
8 and we need to keep guns out of the hands of those who
9 will do harm.

10

11 And we finally need to pass a prohibition on anyone who's
12 on the terrorist watch list from being able to buy a gun in
13 our country. If you're too dangerous to fly, you are too
14 dangerous to buy a gun. So there are things we can do,
15 and we ought to do it in a bipartisan way.

16

17 **HOLT:** Secretary Clinton, last week, you said we've got to
18 do everything possible to improve policing, to go right at
19 implicit bias. Do you believe that police are implicitly
20 biased against black people?

21

22 **CLINTON:** Lester, I think implicit bias is a problem for
23 everyone, not just police. I think, unfortunately, too many
24 of us in our great country jump to conclusions about each
25 other. And therefore, I think we need all of us to be asking
26 hard questions about, you know, why am I feeling this
27 way?

28

29 But when it comes to policing, since it can have literally
30 fatal consequences, I have said, in my first budget, we
31 would put money into that budget to help us deal with
32 implicit bias by retraining a lot of our police officers.

33

1 I've met with a group of very distinguished, experienced
2 police chiefs a few weeks ago. They admit it's an issue.
3 They've got a lot of concerns. Mental health is one of the
4 biggest concerns, because now police are having to handle
5 a lot of really difficult mental health problems on the
6 street.
7
8 **CLINTON:** They want support, they want more training,
9 they want more assistance. And I think the federal
10 government could be in a position where we would offer
11 and provide that.
12
13 **HOLT:** Mr. Trump...
14
15 **TRUMP:** I'd like to respond to that.
16
17 **HOLT:** Please.
18
19 **TRUMP:** First of all, I agree, and a lot of people even within
20 my own party want to give certain rights to people on
21 watch lists and no- fly lists. I agree with you. When a
22 person is on a watch list or a no-fly list, and I have the
23 endorsement of the NRA, which I'm very proud of. These
24 are very, very good people, and they're protecting the
25 Second Amendment.
26
27 But I think we have to look very strongly at no-fly lists and
28 watch lists. And when people are on there, even if they
29 shouldn't be on there, we'll help them, we'll help them
30 legally, we'll help them get off. But I tend to agree with
31 that quite strongly.
32
33 I do want to bring up the fact that you were the one that
34 brought up the words super-predator about young black

1 youth. And that's a term that I think was a -- it's -- it's been
2 horribly met, as you know. I think you've apologized for it.
3 But I think it was a terrible thing to say.
4
5 And when it comes to stop-and-frisk, you know, you're
6 talking about takes guns away. Well, I'm talking about
7 taking guns away from gangs and people that use them.
8 And I don't think -- I really don't think you disagree with
9 me on this, if you want to know the truth.
10
11 I think maybe there's a political reason why you can't say
12 it, but I really don't believe -- in New York City, stop-and-
13 frisk, we had 2,200 murders, and stop-and-frisk brought it
14 down to 500 murders. Five hundred murders is a lot of
15 murders. It's hard to believe, 500 is like supposed to be
16 good?
17
18 But we went from 2,200 to 500. And it was continued on
19 by Mayor Bloomberg. And it was terminated by current
20 mayor. But stop-and- frisk had a tremendous impact on
21 the safety of New York City. Tremendous beyond belief. So
22 when you say it has no impact, it really did. It had a very,
23 very big impact.
24
25 **CLINTON:** Well, it's also fair to say, if we're going to talk
26 about mayors, that under the current mayor, crime has
27 continued to drop, including murders. So there is...
28
29 **TRUMP:** No, you're wrong. You're wrong.
30
31 **CLINTON:** No, I'm not.
32
33 **TRUMP:** Murders are up. All right. You check it.
34

1   **CLINTON:** New York -- New York has done an excellent job.
2   And I give credit -- I give credit across the board going back
3   two mayors, two police chiefs, because it has worked. And
4   other communities need to come together to do what will
5   work, as well.
6
7   Look, one murder is too many. But it is important that we
8   learn about what has been effective. And not go to things
9   that sound good that really did not have the kind of impact
10 that we would want. Who disagrees with keeping
11 neighborhoods safe?
12
13 But let's also add, no one should disagree about respecting
14 the rights of young men who live in those neighborhoods.
15 And so we need to do a better job of working, again, with
16 the   communities,   faith   communities,   business
17 communities, as well as the police to try to deal with this
18 problem.
19
20 **HOLT:** This conversation is about race. And so, Mr. Trump,
21 I have to ask you for five...
22
23 **TRUMP:** I'd like to just respond, if I might.
24
25 **HOLT:** Please -- 20 seconds.
26
27 **TRUMP:** I'd just like to respond.
28
29 **HOLT:** Please respond, then I've got a quick follow-up for
30 you.
31
32 **TRUMP:** I will. Look, the African-American community has
33 been let down by our politicians. They talk good around

1 election time, like right now, and after the election, they
2 said, see ya later, I'll see you in four years.
3
4 The African-American community -- because -- look, the
5 community within the inner cities has been so badly
6 treated. They've been abused and used in order to get
7 votes by Democrat politicians, because that's what it is.
8 They've controlled these communities for up to 100 years.
9
10 **HOLT:** Mr. Trump, let me...
11
12   **(CROSSTALK)**
13
14 **CLINTON:** Well, I -- I do think...
15
16 **TRUMP:** And I will tell you, you look at the inner cities --
17 and I just left Detroit, and I just left Philadelphia, and I just
18 -- you know, you've seen me, I've been all over the place.
19 You decided to stay home, and that's OK. But I will tell you,
20 I've been all over. And I've met some of the greatest
21 people I'll ever meet within these communities. And they
22 are very, very upset with what their politicians have told
23 them and what their politicians have done.
24
25 **HOLT:** Mr. Trump, I...
26
27 **CLINTON:** I think -- I think -- I think Donald just criticized
28 me for preparing for this debate. And, yes, I did. And you
29 know what else I prepared for? I prepared to be president.
30 And I think that's a good thing.
31   **(APPLAUSE)**
32
33 **HOLT:** Mr. Trump, for five years, you perpetuated a false
34 claim that the nation's first black president was not a

1 natural-born citizen. You questioned his legitimacy. In the
2 last couple of weeks, you acknowledged what most
3 Americans have accepted for years: The president was
4 born in the United States. Can you tell us what took you so
5 long?
6
7 **TRUMP:** I'll tell you very -- well, just very simple to say.
8 Sidney Blumenthal works for the campaign and close --
9 very close friend of Secretary Clinton. And her campaign
10 manager, Patti Doyle, went to -- during the campaign, her
11 campaign against President Obama, fought very hard. And
12 you can go look it up, and you can check it out.
13
14 **TRUMP:** And if you look at CNN this past week, Patti Solis
15 Doyle was on Wolf Blitzer saying that this happened.
16 Blumenthal sent McClatchy, highly respected reporter at
17 McClatchy, to Kenya to find out about it. They were
18 pressing it very hard. She failed to get the birth certificate.
19
20 When I got involved, I didn't fail. I got him to give the birth
21 certificate. So I'm satisfied with it. And I'll tell you why I'm
22 satisfied with it.
23
24 **HOLT:** That was...
25
26   **(CROSSTALK)**
27
28 **TRUMP:** Because I want to get on to defeating ISIS,
29 because I want to get on to creating jobs, because I want
30 to get on to having a strong border, because I want to get
31 on to things that are very important to me and that are
32 very important to the country.
33

1 **HOLT:** I will let you respond. It's important. But I just want
2 to get the answer here. The birth certificate was produced
3 in 2011. You've continued to tell the story and question
4 the president's legitimacy in 2012, '13, '14, '15...
5
6 **TRUMP:** Yeah.
7
8 **HOLT:** .... as recently as January. So the question is, what
9 changed your mind?
10
11 **TRUMP:** Well, nobody was pressing it, nobody was caring
12 much about it. I figured you'd ask the question tonight, of
13 course. But nobody was caring much about it. But I was
14 the one that got him to produce the birth certificate. And I
15 think I did a good job.
16
17 Secretary Clinton also fought it. I mean, you know -- now,
18 everybody in mainstream is going to say, oh, that's not
19 true. Look, it's true. Sidney Blumenthal sent a reporter --
20 you just have to take a look at CNN, the last week, the
21 interview with your former campaign manager. And she
22 was involved. But just like she can't bring back jobs, she
23 can't produce.
24
25 **HOLT:** I'm sorry. I'm just going to follow up -- and I will let
26 you respond to that, because there's a lot there. But we're
27 talking about racial healing in this segment. What do you
28 say to Americans, people of color who...
29
30   **(CROSSTALK)**
31
32 **TRUMP:** Well, it was very -- I say nothing. I say nothing,
33 because I was able to get him to produce it. He should
34 have produced it a long time before. I say nothing.

1
2 But let me just tell you. When you talk about healing, I
3 think that I've developed very, very good relationships
4 over the last little while with the African-American
5 community. I think you can see that.
6
7 And I feel that they really wanted me to come to that
8 conclusion. And I think I did a great job and a great service
9 not only for the country, but even for the president, in
10 getting him to produce his birth certificate.
11
12 **HOLT:** Secretary Clinton?
13
14 **CLINTON:** Well, just listen to what you heard.
15
16   **(LAUGHTER)**
17
18 And clearly, as Donald just admitted, he knew he was
19 going to stand on this debate stage, and Lester Holt was
20 going to be asking us questions, so he tried to put the
21 whole racist birther lie to bed.
22
23 But it can't be dismissed that easily. He has really started
24 his political activity based on this racist lie that our first
25 black president was not an American citizen. There was
26 absolutely no evidence for it, but he persisted, he
27 persisted year after year, because some of his supporters,
28 people that he was trying to bring into his fold, apparently
29 believed it or wanted to believe it.
30
31 But, remember, Donald started his career back in 1973
32 being sued by the Justice Department for racial
33 discrimination because he would not rent apartments in
34 one of his developments to African-Americans, and he

1 made sure that the people who worked for him
2 understood that was the policy. He actually was sued
3 twice by the Justice Department.
4
5 So he has a long record of engaging in racist behavior. And
6 the birther lie was a very hurtful one. You know, Barack
7 Obama is a man of great dignity. And I could tell how much
8 it bothered him and annoyed him that this was being
9 touted and used against him.
10
11 But I like to remember what Michelle Obama said in her
12 amazing speech at our Democratic National Convention:
13 When they go low, we go high. And Barack Obama went
14 high, despite Donald Trump's best efforts to bring him
15 down.
16
17 **HOLT:** Mr. Trump, you can respond and we're going to
18 move on to the next segment.
19
20 **TRUMP:** I would love to respond. First of all, I got to watch
21 in preparing for this some of your debates against Barack
22 Obama. You treated him with terrible disrespect. And I
23 watched the way you talk now about how lovely
24 everything is and how wonderful you are. It doesn't work
25 that way. You were after him, you were trying to -- you
26 even sent out or your campaign sent out pictures of him in
27 a certain garb, very famous pictures. I don't think you can
28 deny that.
29
30 But just last week, your campaign manager said it was
31 true. So when you tried to act holier than thou, it really
32 doesn't work. It really doesn't.
33

1   Now, as far as the lawsuit, yes, when I was very young, I
2   went into my father's company, had a real estate company
3   in Brooklyn and Queens, and we, along with many, many
4   other companies throughout the country -- it was a federal
5   lawsuit -- were sued. We settled the suit with zero -- with
6   no admission of guilt. It was very easy to do.
7
8   **TRUMP:** I notice you bring that up a lot. And, you know, I
9   also notice the very nasty commercials that you do on me
10 in so many different ways, which I don't do on you. Maybe
11 I'm trying to save the money.
12
13 But, frankly, I look -- I look at that, and I say, isn't that
14 amazing? Because I settled that lawsuit with no admission
15 of guilt, but that was a lawsuit brought against many real
16 estate firms, and it's just one of those things.
17
18 I'll go one step further. In Palm Beach, Florida, tough
19 community, a brilliant community, a wealthy community,
20 probably the wealthiest community there is in the world, I
21 opened a club, and really got great credit for it. No
22 discrimination against African- Americans, against
23 Muslims, against anybody. And it's a tremendously
24 successful club. And I'm so glad I did it. And I have been
25 given great credit for what I did. And I'm very, very proud
26 of it. And that's the way I feel. That is the true way I feel.
27
28 **HOLT:** Our next segment is called "Securing America." We
29 want to start with a 21st century war happening every day
30 in this country. Our institutions are under cyber attack,
31 and our secrets are being stolen. So my question is, who's
32 behind it? And how do we fight it?
33
34 Secretary Clinton, this answer goes to you.

1
2 **CLINTON:** Well, I think cyber security, cyber warfare will be
3 one of the biggest challenges facing the next president,
4 because clearly we're facing at this point two different
5 kinds of adversaries. There are the independent hacking
6 groups that do it mostly for commercial reasons to try to
7 steal information that they can use to make money.
8
9 But increasingly, we are seeing cyber attacks coming from
10 states, organs of states. The most recent and troubling of
11 these has been Russia. There's no doubt now that Russia
12 has used cyber attacks against all kinds of organizations in
13 our country, and I am deeply concerned about this. I know
14 Donald's very praiseworthy of Vladimir Putin, but Putin is
15 playing a really...
16
17 (CROSSTALK)
18
19 **CLINTON:** ... tough, long game here. And one of the things
20 he's done is to let loose cyber attackers to hack into
21 government files, to hack into personal files, hack into the
22 Democratic National Committee. And we recently have
23 learned that, you know, that this is one of their preferred
24 methods of trying to wreak havoc and collect information.
25 We need to make it very clear -- whether it's Russia, China,
26 Iran or anybody else -- the United States has much greater
27 capacity. And we are not going to sit idly by and permit
28 state actors to go after our information, our private-sector
29 information or our public-sector information.
30
31 And we're going to have to make it clear that we don't
32 want to use the kinds of tools that we have. We don't
33 want to engage in a different kind of warfare. But we will
34 defend the citizens of this country.

1
2 And the Russians need to understand that. I think they've
3 been treating it as almost a probing, how far would we go,
4 how much would we do. And that's why I was so -- I was so
5 shocked when Donald publicly invited Putin to hack into
6 Americans. That is just unacceptable. It's one of the
7 reasons why 50 national security officials who served in
8 Republican information -- in administrations...
9
10 **HOLT:** Your two minutes have expired.
11
12 **CLINTON:** ... have said that Donald is unfit to be the
13 commander- in-chief. It's comments like that that really
14 worry people who understand the threats that we face.
15
16 **HOLT:** Mr. Trump, you have two minutes and the same
17 question. Who's behind it? And how do we fight it?
18
19 **TRUMP:** I do want to say that I was just endorsed -- and
20 more are coming next week -- it will be over 200 admirals,
21 many of them here -- admirals and generals endorsed me
22 to lead this country. That just happened, and many more
23 are coming. And I'm very proud of it.
24
25 In addition, I was just endorsed by ICE. They've never
26 endorsed anybody before on immigration. I was just
27 endorsed by ICE. I was just recently endorsed -- 16,500
28 Border Patrol agents.
29
30 So when Secretary Clinton talks about this, I mean, I'll take
31 the admirals and I'll take the generals any day over the
32 political hacks that I see that have led our country so
33 brilliantly over the last 10 years with their knowledge. OK?

1 Because look at the mess that we're in. Look at the mess
2 that we're in.
3
4 As far as the cyber, I agree to parts of what Secretary
5 Clinton said. We should be better than anybody else, and
6 perhaps we're not. I don't think anybody knows it was
7 Russia that broke into the DNC. She's saying Russia, Russia,
8 Russia, but I don't -- maybe it was. I mean, it could be
9 Russia, but it could also be China. It could also be lots of
10 other people. It also could be somebody sitting on their
11 bed that weighs 400 pounds, OK?
12
13 **TRUMP:** You don't know who broke in to DNC.
14
15 But what did we learn with DNC? We learned that Bernie
16 Sanders was taken advantage of by your people, by Debbie
17 Wasserman Schultz. Look what happened to her. But
18 Bernie Sanders was taken advantage of. That's what we
19 learned.
20
21 Now, whether that was Russia, whether that was China,
22 whether it was another country, we don't know, because
23 the truth is, under President Obama we've lost control of
24 things that we used to have control over.
25
26 We came in with the Internet, we came up with the
27 Internet, and I think Secretary Clinton and myself would
28 agree very much, when you look at what ISIS is doing with
29 the Internet, they're beating us at our own game. ISIS.
30
31 So we have to get very, very tough on cyber and cyber
32 warfare. It is -- it is a huge problem. I have a son. He's 10
33 years old. He has computers. He is so good with these

1 computers, it's unbelievable. The security aspect of cyber
2 is very, very tough. And maybe it's hardly doable.
3
4 But I will say, we are not doing the job we should be doing.
5 But that's true throughout our whole governmental
6 society. We have so many things that we have to do
7 better, Lester, and certainly cyber is one of them.
8
9 **HOLT:** Secretary Clinton?
10
11 **CLINTON:** Well, I think there are a number of issues that
12 we should be addressing. I have put forth a plan to defeat
13 ISIS. It does involve going after them online. I think we
14 need to do much more with our tech companies to
15 prevent ISIS and their operatives from being able to use
16 the Internet to radicalize, even direct people in our
17 country and Europe and elsewhere.
18
19 But we also have to intensify our air strikes against ISIS
20 and eventually support our Arab and Kurdish partners to
21 be able to actually take out ISIS in Raqqa, end their claim
22 of being a Caliphate.
23
24 We're making progress. Our military is assisting in Iraq.
25 And we're hoping that within the year we'll be able to
26 push ISIS out of Iraq and then, you know, really squeeze
27 them in Syria.
28
29 But we have to be cognizant of the fact that they've had
30 foreign fighters coming to volunteer for them, foreign
31 money, foreign weapons, so we have to make this the top
32 priority.
33

1 And I would also do everything possible to take out their
2 leadership. I was involved in a number of efforts to take
3 out Al Qaida leadership when I was secretary of state,
4 including, of course, taking out bin Laden. And I think we
5 need to go after Baghdadi, as well, make that one of our
6 organizing principles. Because we've got to defeat ISIS, and
7 we've got to do everything we can to disrupt their
8 propaganda efforts online.
9
10 **HOLT:** You mention ISIS, and we think of ISIS certainly as
11 over there, but there are American citizens who have been
12 inspired to commit acts of terror on American soil, the
13 latest incident, of course, the bombings we just saw in
14 New York and New Jersey, the knife attack at a mall in
15 Minnesota, in the last year, deadly attacks in San
16 Bernardino and Orlando. I'll ask this to both of you. Tell us
17 specifically how you would prevent homegrown attacks by
18 American citizens, Mr. Trump?
19
20 **TRUMP:** Well, first I have to say one thing, very important.
21 Secretary Clinton is talking about taking out ISIS. "We will
22 take out ISIS." Well, President Obama and Secretary
23 Clinton created a vacuum the way they got out of Iraq,
24 because they got out -- what, they shouldn't have been in,
25 but once they got in, the way they got out was a disaster.
26 And ISIS was formed.
27
28 So she talks about taking them out. She's been doing it a
29 long time. She's been trying to take them out for a long
30 time. But they wouldn't have even been formed if they left
31 some troops behind, like 10,000 or maybe something
32 more than that. And then you wouldn't have had them.
33

1 Or, as I've been saying for a long time, and I think you'll
2 agree, because I said it to you once, had we taken the oil --
3 and we should have taken the oil -- ISIS would not have
4 been able to form either, because the oil was their primary
5 source of income. And now they have the oil all over the
6 place, including the oil -- a lot of the oil in Libya, which was
7 another one of her disasters.
8
9 **HOLT:** Secretary Clinton?
10
11 **CLINTON:** Well, I hope the fact-checkers are turning up the
12 volume and really working hard. Donald supported the
13 invasion of Iraq.
14
15 **TRUMP:** Wrong.
16
17 **CLINTON:** That is absolutely proved over and over again.
18
19 **TRUMP:** Wrong. Wrong.
20
21 **CLINTON:** He actually advocated for the actions we took in
22 Libya and urged that Gadhafi be taken out, after actually
23 doing some business with him one time.
24
25 **CLINTON:** But the larger point -- and he says this
26 constantly -- is George W. Bush made the agreement
27 about when American troops would leave Iraq, not Barack
28 Obama.
29
30 And the only way that American troops could have stayed
31 in Iraq is to get an agreement from the then-Iraqi
32 government that would have protected our troops, and
33 the Iraqi government would not give that.
34

1 But let's talk about the question you asked, Lester. The
2 question you asked is, what do we do here in the United
3 States? That's the most important part of this. How do we
4 prevent attacks? How do we protect our people?
5
6 And I think we've got to have an intelligence surge, where
7 we are looking for every scrap of information. I was so
8 proud of law enforcement in New York, in Minnesota, in
9 New Jersey. You know, they responded so quickly, so
10 professionally to the attacks that occurred by Rahami. And
11 they brought him down. And we may find out more
12 information because he is still alive, which may prove to
13 be an intelligence benefit.
14
15 So we've got to do everything we can to vacuum up
16 intelligence from Europe, from the Middle East. That
17 means we've got to work more closely with our allies, and
18 that's something that Donald has been very dismissive of.
19
20 We're working with NATO, the longest military alliance in
21 the history of the world, to really turn our attention to
22 terrorism. We're working with our friends in the Middle
23 East, many of which, as you know, are Muslim majority
24 nations. Donald has consistently insulted Muslims abroad,
25 Muslims at home, when we need to be cooperating with
26 Muslim nations and with the American Muslim
27 community.
28
29 They're on the front lines. They can provide information to
30 us that we might not get anywhere else. They need to
31 have close working cooperation with law enforcement in
32 these communities, not be alienated and pushed away as
33 some of Donald's rhetoric, unfortunately, has led to.
34

1 **HOLT:** Mr. Trump...

2

3 **TRUMP:** Well, I have to respond.

4

5 **HOLT:** Please respond.

6

7 **TRUMP:** The secretary said very strongly about working
8 with -- we've been working with them for many years, and
9 we have the greatest mess anyone's ever seen. You look at
10 the Middle East, it's a total mess. Under your direction, to
11 a large extent.

12

13 But you look at the Middle East, you started the Iran deal,
14 that's another beauty where you have a country that was
15 ready to fall, I mean, they were doing so badly. They were
16 choking on the sanctions. And now they're going to be
17 actually probably a major power at some point pretty
18 soon, the way they're going.

19

20 But when you look at NATO, I was asked on a major show,
21 what do you think of NATO? And you have to understand,
22 I'm a businessperson. I did really well. But I have common
23 sense. And I said, well, I'll tell you. I haven't given lots of
24 thought to NATO. But two things.

25

26 Number one, the 28 countries of NATO, many of them
27 aren't paying their fair share. Number two -- and that
28 bothers me, because we should be asking -- we're
29 defending them, and they should at least be paying us
30 what they're supposed to be paying by treaty and
31 contract.

32

33 And, number two, I said, and very strongly, NATO could be
34 obsolete, because -- and I was very strong on this, and it

1 was actually covered very accurately in the New York
2 Times, which is unusual for the New York Times, to be
3 honest -- but I said, they do not focus on terror. And I was
4 very strong. And I said it numerous times.
5
6 And about four months ago, I read on the front page of the
7 Wall Street Journal that NATO is opening up a major terror
8 division. And I think that's great. And I think we should get
9 -- because we pay approximately 73 percent of the cost of
10 NATO. It's a lot of money to protect other people. But I'm
11 all for NATO. But I said they have to focus on terror, also.
12
13 And they're going to do that. And that was -- believe me --
14 I'm sure I'm not going to get credit for it -- but that was
15 largely because of what I was saying and my criticism of
16 NATO.
17
18 I think we have to get NATO to go into the Middle East
19 with us, in addition to surrounding nations, and we have to
20 knock the hell out of ISIS, and we have to do it fast, when
21 ISIS formed in this vacuum created by Barack Obama and
22 Secretary Clinton. And believe me, you were the ones that
23 took out the troops. Not only that, you named the day.
24 They couldn't believe it. They sat back probably and said, I
25 can't believe it. They said...
26
27 **CLINTON:** Lester, we've covered...
28
29 **TRUMP:** No, wait a minute.
30
31 **CLINTON:** We've covered this ground.
32
33 **TRUMP:** When they formed, when they formed, this is
34 something that never should have happened. It should

1 have never happened. Now, you're talking about taking
2 out ISIS. But you were there, and you were secretary of
3 state when it was a little infant. Now it's in over 30
4 countries. And you're going to stop them? I don't think so.
5
6 **HOLT:** Mr. Trump, a lot of these are judgment questions.
7 You had supported the war in Iraq before the invasion.
8 What makes your...
9
10 **TRUMP:** I did not support the war in Iraq.
11
12 **HOLT:** In 2002...
13
14 **TRUMP:** That is a mainstream media nonsense put out by
15 her, because she -- frankly, I think the best person in her
16 campaign is mainstream media.
17
18 **HOLT:** My question is, since you supported it...
19
20 **TRUMP:** Just -- would you like to hear...
21
22 **HOLT:** ... why is your -- why is your judgment...
23
24 **TRUMP:** Wait a minute. I was against the war in Iraq. Just
25 so you put it out.
26
27 **HOLT:** The record shows otherwise, but why -- why was...
28
29 **TRUMP:** The record does not show that.
30
31 **HOLT:** Why was -- is your judgment any...
32
33 **TRUMP:** The record shows that I'm right. When I did an
34 interview with Howard Stern, very lightly, first time

1 anyone's asked me that, I said, very lightly, I don't know,
2 maybe, who knows? Essentially. I then did an interview
3 with Neil Cavuto. We talked about the economy is more
4 important. I then spoke to Sean Hannity, which everybody
5 refuses to call Sean Hannity. I had numerous conversations
6 with Sean Hannity at Fox. And Sean Hannity said -- and he
7 called me the other day -- and I spoke to him about it -- he
8 said you were totally against the war, because he was for
9 the war.
10
11 **HOLT:** Why is your judgment better than...
12
13 **TRUMP:** And when he -- excuse me. And that was before
14 the war started. Sean Hannity said very strongly to me and
15 other people -- he's willing to say it, but nobody wants to
16 call him. I was against the war. He said, you used to have
17 fights with me, because Sean was in favor of the war.
18
19 And I understand that side, also, not very much, because
20 we should have never been there. But nobody called Sean
21 Hannity. And then they did an article in a major magazine,
22 shortly after the war started. I think in '04. But they did an
23 article which had me totally against the war in Iraq.
24
25 And one of your compatriots said, you know, whether it
26 was before or right after, Trump was definitely -- because
27 if you read this article, there's no doubt. But if somebody -
28 - and I'll ask the press -- if somebody would call up Sean
29 Hannity, this was before the war started. He and I used to
30 have arguments about the war. I said, it's a terrible and a
31 stupid thing. It's going to destabilize the Middle East. And
32 that's exactly what it's done. It's been a disaster.
33

1 **HOLT:** My reference was to what you had said in 2002, and
2 my question was...
3
4 **TRUMP:** No, no. You didn't hear what I said.
5
6 **HOLT:** Why is your judgment -- why is your judgment any
7 different than Mrs. Clinton's judgment?
8
9 **TRUMP:** Well, I have much better judgment than she does.
10 There's no question about that. I also have a much better
11 temperament than she has, you know?
12
13   **(LAUGHTER)**
14
15 I have a much better -- she spent -- let me tell you -- she
16 spent hundreds of millions of dollars on an advertising --
17 you know, they get Madison Avenue into a room, they put
18 names -- oh, temperament, let's go after -- I think my
19 strongest asset, maybe by far, is my temperament. I have a
20 winning temperament. I know how to win. She does not
21 have a...
22
23 **HOLT:** Secretary Clinton?
24
25 **TRUMP:** Wait. The AFL-CIO the other day, behind the blue
26 screen, I don't know who you were talking to, Secretary
27 Clinton, but you were totally out of control. I said, there's a
28 person with a temperament that's got a problem.
29
30 **HOLT:** Secretary Clinton?
31
32 **CLINTON:** Whew, OK.
33
34 (LAUGHTER)

1
2 Let's talk about two important issues that were briefly
3 mentioned by Donald, first, NATO. You know, NATO as a
4 military alliance has something called Article 5, and
5 basically it says this: An attack on one is an attack on all.
6 And you know the only time it's ever been invoked? After
7 9/11, when the 28 nations of NATO said that they would
8 go to Afghanistan with us to fight terrorism, something
9 that they still are doing by our side.
10
11 With respect to Iran, when I became secretary of state,
12 Iran was weeks away from having enough nuclear material
13 to form a bomb. They had mastered the nuclear fuel cycle
14 under the Bush administration. They had built covert
15 facilities. They had stocked them with centrifuges that
16 were whirling away.
17
18 And we had sanctioned them. I voted for every sanction
19 against Iran when I was in the Senate, but it wasn't
20 enough. So I spent a year-and-a-half putting together a
21 coalition that included Russia and China to impose the
22 toughest sanctions on Iran.
23
24 And we did drive them to the negotiating table. And my
25 successor, John Kerry, and President Obama got a deal
26 that put a lid on Iran's nuclear program without firing a
27 single shot. That's diplomacy. That's coalition-building.
28 That's working with other nations.
29
30 The other day, I saw Donald saying that there were some
31 Iranian sailors on a ship in the waters off of Iran, and they
32 were taunting American sailors who were on a nearby
33 ship. He said, you know, if they taunted our sailors, I'd

1 blow them out of the water and start another war. That's
2 not good judgment.
3
4 **TRUMP:** That would not start a war.
5
6 **CLINTON:** That is not the right temperament to be
7 commander-in- chief, to be taunted. And the worst part...
8
9 **TRUMP:** No, they were taunting us.
10
11 **CLINTON:** ... of what we heard Donald say has been about
12 nuclear weapons. He has said repeatedly that he didn't
13 care if other nations got nuclear weapons, Japan, South
14 Korea, even Saudi Arabia. It has been the policy of the
15 United States, Democrats and Republicans, to do
16 everything we could to reduce the proliferation of nuclear
17 weapons. He even said, well, you know, if there were
18 nuclear war in East Asia, well, you know, that's fine...
19
20 **TRUMP:** Wrong.
21
22 **CLINTON:** ... have a good time, folks.
23
24 **TRUMP:** It's lies.
25
26 **CLINTON:** And, in fact, his cavalier attitude about nuclear
27 weapons is so deeply troubling. That is the number-one
28 threat we face in the world. And it becomes particularly
29 threatening if terrorists ever get their hands on any
30 nuclear material. So a man who can be provoked by a
31 tweet should not have his fingers anywhere near the
32 nuclear codes, as far as I think anyone with any sense
33 about this should be concerned.
34

1 **TRUMP:** That line's getting a little bit old, I must say. I
2 would like to...
3
4 **CLINTON:** It's a good one, though. It well describes the
5 problem.
6
7 (LAUGHTER)
8
9 **TRUMP:** It's not an accurate one at all. It's not an accurate
10 one. So I just want to give a lot of things -- and just to
11 respond. I agree with her on one thing. The single greatest
12 problem the world has is nuclear armament, nuclear
13 weapons, not global warming, like you think and your --
14 your president thinks.
15
16 Nuclear is the single greatest threat. Just to go down the
17 list, we defend Japan, we defend Germany, we defend
18 South Korea, we defend Saudi Arabia, we defend
19 countries. They do not pay us. But they should be paying
20 us, because we are providing tremendous service and
21 we're losing a fortune. That's why we're losing -- we're
22 losing -- we lose on everything. I say, who makes these --
23 we lose on everything. All I said, that it's very possible that
24 if they don't pay a fair share, because this isn't 40 years
25 ago where we could do what we're doing. We can't defend
26 Japan, a behemoth, selling us cars by the million...
27
28 **HOLT:** We need to move on.
29
30 **TRUMP:** Well, wait, but it's very important. All I said was,
31 they may have to defend themselves or they have to help
32 us out. We're a country that owes $20 trillion. They have
33 to help us out.
34

1 **HOLT:** Our last...

2

3 **TRUMP:** As far as the nuclear is concerned, I agree. It is the
4 single greatest threat that this country has.

5

6 **HOLT:** Which leads to my next question, as we enter our
7 last segment here (inaudible) the subject of securing
8 America. On nuclear weapons, President Obama
9 reportedly considered changing the nation's longstanding
10 policy on first use. Do you support the current policy? Mr.
11 Trump, you have two minutes on that.

12

13 **TRUMP:** Well, I have to say that, you know, for what
14 Secretary Clinton was saying about nuclear with Russia,
15 she's very cavalier in the way she talks about various
16 countries. But Russia has been expanding their -- they
17 have a much newer capability than we do. We have not
18 been updating from the new standpoint.

19

20 I looked the other night. I was seeing B-52s, they're old
21 enough that your father, your grandfather could be flying
22 them. We are not -- we are not keeping up with other
23 countries. I would like everybody to end it, just get rid of
24 it. But I would certainly not do first strike.

25

26 I think that once the nuclear alternative happens, it's over.
27 At the same time, we have to be prepared. I can't take
28 anything off the table. Because you look at some of these
29 countries, you look at North Korea, we're doing nothing
30 there. China should solve that problem for us. China
31 should go into North Korea. China is totally powerful as it
32 relates to North Korea.

33

1 And by the way, another one powerful is the worst deal I
2 think I've ever seen negotiated that you started is the Iran
3 deal. Iran is one of their biggest trading partners. Iran has
4 power over North Korea.
5
6 And when they made that horrible deal with Iran, they
7 should have included the fact that they do something with
8 respect to North Korea. And they should have done
9 something with respect to Yemen and all these other
10 places.
11
12 And when asked to Secretary Kerry, why didn't you do
13 that? Why didn't you add other things into the deal? One
14 of the great giveaways of all time, of all time, including
15 $400 million in cash. Nobody's ever seen that before. That
16 turned out to be wrong. It was actually $1.7 billion in cash,
17 obviously, I guess for the hostages. It certainly looks that
18 way.
19
20 So you say to yourself, why didn't they make the right
21 deal? This is one of the worst deals ever made by any
22 country in history. The deal with Iran will lead to nuclear
23 problems. All they have to do is sit back 10 years, and they
24 don't have to do much.
25
26 **HOLT:** Your two minutes is expired.
27
28 **TRUMP:** And they're going to end up getting nuclear. I met
29 with Bibi Netanyahu the other day. Believe me, he's not a
30 happy camper.
31
32 **HOLT:** All right. Mrs. Clinton, Secretary Clinton, you have
33 two minutes.
34

1 **CLINTON:** Well, let me -- let me start by saying, words
2 matter. Words matter when you run for president. And
3 they really matter when you are president. And I want to
4 reassure our allies in Japan and South Korea and
5 elsewhere that we have mutual defense treaties and we
6 will honor them.
7
8 It is essential that America's word be good. And so I know
9 that this campaign has caused some questioning and
10 worries on the part of many leaders across the globe. I've
11 talked with a number of them. But I want to -- on behalf of
12 myself, and I think on behalf of a majority of the American
13 people, say that, you know, our word is good.
14
15 It's also important that we look at the entire global
16 situation. There's no doubt that we have other problems
17 with Iran. But personally, I'd rather deal with the other
18 problems having put that lid on their nuclear program than
19 still to be facing that.
20
21 And Donald never tells you what he would do. Would he
22 have started a war? Would he have bombed Iran? If he's
23 going to criticize a deal that has been very successful in
24 giving us access to Iranian facilities that we never had
25 before, then he should tell us what his alternative would
26 be. But it's like his plan to defeat ISIS. He says it's a secret
27 plan, but the only secret is that he has no plan.
28
29 So we need to be more precise in how we talk about these
30 issues. People around the word follow our presidential
31 campaigns so closely, trying to get hints about what we
32 will do. Can they rely on us? Are we going to lead the
33 world with strength and in accordance with our values?
34 That's what I intend to do. I intend to be a leader of our

1 country that people can count on, both here at home and
2 around the world, to make decisions that will further
3 peace and prosperity, but also stand up to bullies, whether
4 they're abroad or at home.
5
6 We cannot let those who would try to destabilize the
7 world to interfere with American interests and security...
8
9 **HOLT:** Your two minutes is...
10
11 **CLINTON:** ... to be given any opportunities at all.
12
13 **HOLT:** ... is expired.
14
15 **TRUMP:** Lester, one thing I'd like to say.
16
17 **HOLT:** Very quickly. Twenty seconds.
18
19 **TRUMP:** I will go very quickly. But I will tell you that Hillary
20 will tell you to go to her website and read all about how to
21 defeat ISIS, which she could have defeated by never
22 having it, you know, get going in the first place. Right now,
23 it's getting tougher and tougher to defeat them, because
24 they're in more and more places, more and more states,
25 more and more nations.
26
27 **HOLT:** Mr. Trump...
28
29 **TRUMP:** And it's a big problem. And as far as Japan is
30 concerned, I want to help all of our allies, but we are losing
31 billions and billions of dollars. We cannot be the policemen
32 of the world. We cannot protect countries all over the
33 world...
34

1 **HOLT:** We have just...

2

3 **TRUMP:** ... where they're not paying us what we need.

4

5 **HOLT:** We have just a few final questions...

6

7 **TRUMP:** And she doesn't say that, because she's got no
8 business ability. We need heart. We need a lot of things.
9 But you have to have some basic ability. And sadly, she
10 doesn't have that. All of the things that she's talking about
11 could have been taken care of during the last 10 years,
12 let's say, while she had great power. But they weren't
13 taken care of. And if she ever wins this race, they won't be
14 taken care of.

15

16 **HOLT:** Mr. Trump, this year Secretary Clinton became the
17 first woman nominated for president by a major party.
18 Earlier this month, you said she doesn't have, quote, "a
19 presidential look." She's standing here right now. What did
20 you mean by that?

21

22 **TRUMP:** She doesn't have the look. She doesn't have the
23 stamina. I said she doesn't have the stamina. And I don't
24 believe she does have the stamina. To be president of this
25 country, you need tremendous stamina.

26

27 **HOLT:** The quote was, "I just don't think she has the
28 presidential look."

29

30 **TRUMP:** You have -- wait a minute. Wait a minute, Lester.
31 You asked me a question. Did you ask me a question?

32

33 You have to be able to negotiate our trade deals. You have
34 to be able to negotiate, that's right, with Japan, with Saudi

1 Arabia. I mean, can you imagine, we're defending Saudi
2 Arabia? And with all of the money they have, we're
3 defending them, and they're not paying? All you have to
4 do is speak to them. Wait. You have so many different
5 things you have to be able to do, and I don't believe that
6 Hillary has the stamina.
7
8 **HOLT:** Let's let her respond.
9
10 **CLINTON:** Well, as soon as he travels to 112 countries and
11 negotiates a peace deal, a cease-fire, a release of
12 dissidents, an opening of new opportunities in nations
13 around the world, or even spends 11 hours testifying in
14 front of a congressional committee, he can talk to me
15 about stamina.
16
17   **(APPLAUSE)**
18
19 **TRUMP:** The world -- let me tell you. Let me tell you.
20 Hillary has experience, but it's bad experience. We have
21 made so many bad deals during the last -- so she's got
22 experience, that I agree.
23
24 **(APPLAUSE)**
25
26 But it's bad, bad experience. Whether it's the Iran deal
27 that you're so in love with, where we gave them $150
28 billion back, whether it's the Iran deal, whether it's
29 anything you can -- name -- you almost can't name a good
30 deal. I agree. She's got experience, but it's bad experience.
31 And this country can't afford to have another four years of
32 that kind of experience.
33
34 **HOLT:** We are at -- we are at the final question.

1
2 **(APPLAUSE)**
3
4 **CLINTON:** Well, one thing. One thing, Lester.
5
6 **HOLT:** Very quickly, because we're at the final question
7 now.
8
9 **CLINTON:** You know, he tried to switch from looks to
10 stamina. But this is a man who has called women pigs,
11 slobs and dogs, and someone who has said pregnancy is an
12 inconvenience to employers, who has said...
13
14 **TRUMP:** I never said that.
15
16 **CLINTON:** .... women don't deserve equal pay unless they
17 do as good a job as men.
18
19 **TRUMP:** I didn't say that.
20
21 **CLINTON:** And one of the worst things he said was about a
22 woman in a beauty contest. He loves beauty contests,
23 supporting them and hanging around them. And he called
24 this woman "Miss Piggy." Then he called her "Miss
25 Housekeeping," because she was Latina. Donald, she has a
26 name.
27
28 **TRUMP:** Where did you find this? Where did you find this?
29
30 **CLINTON:** Her name is Alicia Machado.
31
32 **TRUMP:** Where did you find this?
33

1 **CLINTON:** And she has become a U.S. citizen, and you can
2 bet...
3
4 **TRUMP:** Oh, really? **CLINTON:** ... she's going to vote this
5 November.
6
7 **TRUMP:** OK, good. Let me just tell you...
8
9 **(APPLAUSE)**
10
11 **HOLT:** Mr. Trump, could we just take 10 seconds and then
12 we ask the final question...
13
14 **TRUMP:** You know; Hillary is hitting me with tremendous
15 commercials. Some of it's said in entertainment. Some of
16 it's said -- somebody who's been very vicious to me, Rosie
17 O'Donnell, I said very tough things to her, and I think
18 everybody would agree that she deserves it and nobody
19 feels sorry for her.
20
21 But you want to know the truth? I was going to say
22 something...
23
24 **HOLT:** Please very quickly.
25
26 **TRUMP:** ... extremely rough to Hillary, to her family, and I
27 said to myself, "I can't do it. I just can't do it. It's
28 inappropriate. It's not nice." But she spent hundreds of
29 millions of dollars on negative ads on me, many of which
30 are absolutely untrue. They're untrue. And they're
31 misrepresentations.
32
33 And I will tell you this, Lester: It's not nice. And I don't
34 deserve that.

1
2 But it's certainly not a nice thing that she's done. It's
3 hundreds of millions of ads. And the only gratifying thing
4 is, I saw the polls come in today, and with all of that
5 money...
6
7 **HOLT:** We have to move on to the final question.
8
9 **TRUMP:** ... $200 million is spent, and I'm either winning or
10 tied, and I've spent practically nothing.
11
12 **(APPLAUSE)**
13
14 **HOLT:** One of you will not win this election. So my final
15 question to you tonight, are you willing to accept the
16 outcome as the will of the voters? Secretary Clinton?
17
18 **CLINTON:** Well, I support our democracy. And sometimes
19 you win, sometimes you lose. But I certainly will support
20 the outcome of this election.
21
22 And I know Donald's trying very hard to plant doubts
23 about it, but I hope the people out there understand: This
24 election's really up to you. It's not about us so much as it is
25 about you and your families and the kind of country and
26 future you want. So I sure hope you will get out and vote
27 as though your future depended on it, because I think it
28 does.
29
30 **HOLT:** Mr. Trump, very quickly, same question. Will you
31 accept the outcome as the will of the voters?
32

1　**TRUMP:** I want to make America great again. We are a
2　nation that is seriously troubled. We're losing our jobs.
3　People are pouring into our country.
4
5　The other day, we were deporting 800 people. And
6　perhaps they passed the wrong button, they pressed the
7　wrong button, or perhaps worse than that, it was
8　corruption, but these people that we were going to deport
9　for good reason ended up becoming citizens. Ended up
10　becoming citizens. And it was 800. And now it turns out it
11　might be 1,800, and they don't even know.
12
13　**HOLT:** Will you accept the outcome of the election?
14
15　**TRUMP:** Look, here's the story. I want to make America
16　great again. I'm going to be able to do it. I don't believe
17　Hillary will. The answer is, if she wins, I will absolutely
18　support her.
19
20　**(APPLAUSE)**
21
22　**HOLT:** All right. Well, that is going to do it for us. That
23　concludes our debate for this evening, a spirit one. We
24　covered a lot of ground, not everything as I suspected we
25　would.

SECOND

PRESIDENTIAL

DEBATE

1 **RADDATZ:** Ladies and gentlemen the Republican nominee
2 for president, Donald J. Trump, and the Democratic
3 nominee for president, Hillary Clinton.
4
5 **(APPLAUSE)**
6
7 **COOPER:** Thank you very much for being here. We're
8 going to begin with a question from one of the members in
9 our town hall. Each of you will have two minutes to
10 respond to this question. Secretary Clinton, you won the
11 coin toss, so you'll go first. Our first question comes from
12 Patrice Brock. Patrice?
13
14 QUESTION: Thank you, and good evening. The last debate
15 could have been rated as MA, mature audiences, per TV
16 parental guidelines. Knowing that educators assign viewing
17 the presidential debates as students' homework, do you
18 feel you're modeling appropriate and positive behavior for
19 today's youth?
20
21
22 Continue reading the main story
23

75

1 **<u>CLINTON:</u>** Well, thank you. Are you a teacher? Yes, I think
2 that that's a very good question, because I've heard from
3 lots of teachers and parents about some of their concerns
4 about some of the things that are being said and done in
5 this campaign.
6
7 And I think it is very important for us to make clear to our
8 children that our country really is great because we're
9 good. And we are going to respect one another, lift each
10 other up. We are going to be looking for ways to celebrate
11 our diversity, and we are going to try to reach out to every
12 boy and girl, as well as every adult, to bring them in to
13 working on behalf of our country.
14
15 I have a very positive and optimistic view about what we
16 can do together. That's why the slogan of my campaign is
17 "Stronger Together," because I think if we work together,
18 if we overcome the divisiveness that sometimes sets
19 Americans against one another, and instead we make
20 some big goals — and I've set forth some big goals, getting
21 the economy to work for everyone, not just those at the
22 top, making sure that we have the best education system
23 from preschool through college and making it affordable,
24 and so much else.
25
26 If we set those goals and we go together to try to achieve
27 them, there's nothing in my opinion that America can't do.
28 So that's why I hope that we will come together in this
29 campaign. Obviously, I'm hoping to earn your vote, I'm
30 hoping to be elected in November, and I can promise you,
31 I will work with every American.
32
33 I want to be the president for all Americans, regardless of
34 your political beliefs, where you come from, what you look

1 like, your religion. I want us to heal our country and bring
2 it together because that's, I think, the best way for us to
3 get the future that our children and our grandchildren
4 deserve.
5
6 **COOPER:** Secretary Clinton, thank you. Mr. Trump, you
7 have two minutes.
8
9 **TRUMP:** Well, I actually agree with that. I agree with
10 everything she said. I began this campaign because I was
11 so tired of seeing such foolish things happen to our
12 country. This is a great country. This is a great land. I've
13 gotten to know the people of the country over the last
14 year-and-a-half that I've been doing this as a politician. I
15 cannot believe I'm saying that about myself, but I guess I
16 have been a politician.
17
18 **TRUMP:** And my whole concept was to make America
19 great again. When I watch the deals being made, when I
20 watch what's happening with some horrible things like
21 Obamacare, where your health insurance and health care
22 is going up by numbers that are astronomical, 68 percent,
23 59 percent, 71 percent, when I look at the Iran deal and
24 how bad a deal it is for us, it's a one-sided transaction
25 where we're giving back $150 billion to a terrorist state,
26 really, the number one terror state, we've made them a
27 strong country from really a very weak country just three
28 years ago.
29
30 When I look at all of the things that I see and all of the
31 potential that our country has, we have such tremendous
32 potential, whether it's in business and trade, where we're
33 doing so badly. Last year, we had almost $800 billion trade
34 deficit. In other words, trading with other countries. We

1 had an $800 billion deficit. It's hard to believe.
2 Inconceivable.
3
4 You say who's making these deals? We're going the make
5 great deals. We're going to have a strong border. We're
6 going to bring back law and order. Just today, policemen
7 was shot, two killed. And this is happening on a weekly
8 basis. We have to bring back respect to law enforcement.
9 At the same time, we have to take care of people on all
10 sides. We need justice.
11
12 But I want to do things that haven't been done, including
13 fixing and making our inner cities better for the African-
14 American citizens that are so great, and for the Latinos,
15 Hispanics, and I look forward to doing it. It's called make
16 America great again.
17
18 **COOPER:** Thank you, Mr. Trump. The question from
19 Patrice was about are you both modeling positive and
20 appropriate behavior for today's youth? We received a lot
21 of questions online, Mr. Trump, about the tape that was
22 released on Friday, as you can imagine. You called what
23 you said locker room banter. You described kissing women
24 without consent, grabbing their genitals. That is sexual
25 assault. You bragged that you have sexually assaulted
26 women. Do you understand that?
27
28 **TRUMP:** No, I didn't say that at all. I don't think you
29 understood what was — this was locker room talk. I'm not
30 proud of it. I apologize to my family. I apologize to the
31 American people. Certainly I'm not proud of it. But this is
32 locker room talk.
33

1 You know, when we have a world where you have ISIS
2 chopping off heads, where you have — and, frankly,
3 drowning people in steel cages, where you have wars and
4 horrible, horrible sights all over, where you have so many
5 bad things happening, this is like medieval times. We
6 haven't seen anything like this, the carnage all over the
7 world.
8
9 And they look and they see. Can you imagine the people
10 that are, frankly, doing so well against us with ISIS? And
11 they look at our country and they see what's going on.
12
13 Yes, I'm very embarrassed by it. I hate it. But it's locker
14 room talk, and it's one of those things. I will knock the hell
15 out of ISIS. We're going to defeat ISIS. ISIS happened a
16 number of years ago in a vacuum that was left because of
17 bad judgment. And I will tell you, I will take care of ISIS.
18
19 **COOPER:** So, Mr. Trump...
20
21 **TRUMP:** And we should get on to much more important
22 things and much bigger things.
23
24 **COOPER:** Just for the record, though, are you saying that
25 what you said on that bus 11 years ago that you did not
26 actually kiss women without consent or grope women
27 without consent?
28
29 **TRUMP:** I have great respect for women. Nobody has
30 more respect for women than I do.
31
32 **COOPER:** So, for the record, you're saying you never did
33 that?
34

1 **TRUMP:** I've said things that, frankly, you hear these
2 things I said. And I was embarrassed by it. But I have
3 tremendous respect for women.
4
5 **COOPER:** Have you ever done those things?
6
7 **TRUMP:** And women have respect for me. And I will tell
8 you: No, I have not. And I will tell you that I'm going to
9 make our country safe. We're going to have borders in our
10 country, which we don't have now. People are pouring
11 into our country, and they're coming in from the Middle
12 East and other places.
13
14 We're going to make America safe again. We're going to
15 make America great again, but we're going to make
16 America safe again. And we're going to make America
17 wealthy again, because if you don't do that, it just — it
18 sounds harsh to say, but we have to build up the wealth of
19 our nation.
20
21 **COOPER:** Thank you, Mr. Trump.
22
23 **TRUMP:** Right now, other nations are taking our jobs and
24 they're taking our wealth.
25
26 **COOPER:** Thank you, Mr. Trump.
27
28 **TRUMP:** And that's what I want to talk about.
29
30 **COOPER:** Secretary Clinton, do you want to respond?
31
32 **CLINTON:** Well, like everyone else, I've spent a lot of time
33 thinking over the last 48 hours about what we heard and
34 saw. You know, with prior Republican nominees for

1 president, I disagreed with them on politics, policies,
2 principles, but I never questioned their fitness to serve.
3
4 Donald Trump is different. I said starting back in June that
5 he was not fit to be president and commander-in-chief.
6 And many Republicans and independents have said the
7 same thing. What we all saw and heard on Friday was
8 Donald talking about women, what he thinks about
9 women, what he does to women. And he has said that the
10 video doesn't represent who he is.
11
12 But I think it's clear to anyone who heard it that it
13 represents exactly who he is. Because we've seen this
14 throughout the campaign. We have seen him insult
15 women. We've seen him rate women on their appearance,
16 ranking them from one to ten. We've seen him embarrass
17 women on TV and on Twitter. We saw him after the first
18 debate spend nearly a week denigrating a former Miss
19 Universe in the harshest, most personal terms.
20
21 So, yes, this is who Donald Trump is. But it's not only
22 women, and it's not only this video that raises questions
23 about his fitness to be our president, because he has also
24 targeted immigrants, African- Americans, Latinos, people
25 with disabilities, POWs, Muslims, and so many others.
26
27 So this is who Donald Trump is. And the question for us,
28 the question our country must answer is that this is not
29 who we are. That's why — to go back to your question — I
30 want to send a message — we all should — to every boy
31 and girl and, indeed, to the entire world that America
32 already is great, but we are great because we are good,
33 and we will respect one another, and we will work with
34 one another, and we will celebrate our diversity.

1
2 **CLINTON:** These are very important values to me, because
3 this is the America that I know and love. And I can pledge
4 to you tonight that this is the America that I will serve if
5 I'm so fortunate enough to become your president.
6
7 **RADDATZ:** And we want to get to some questions from
8 online...
9
10 **TRUMP:** Am I allowed to respond to that? I assume I am.
11
12 **RADDATZ:** Yes, you can respond to that.
13
14 **TRUMP:** It's just words, folks. It's just words. Those words,
15 I've been hearing them for many years. I heard them when
16 they were running for the Senate in New York, where
17 Hillary was going to bring back jobs to upstate New York
18 and she failed.
19
20 I've heard them where Hillary is constantly talking about
21 the inner cities of our country, which are a disaster
22 education-wise, jobwise, safety-wise, in every way
23 possible. I'm going to help the African-Americans. I'm
24 going to help the Latinos, Hispanics. I am going to help the
25 inner cities.
26
27 She's done a terrible job for the African-Americans. She
28 wants their vote, and she does nothing, and then she
29 comes back four years later. We saw that firsthand when
30 she was United States senator. She campaigned where the
31 primary part of her campaign...
32
33 **RADDATZ:** Mr. Trump, Mr. Trump — I want to get to
34 audience questions and online questions.

1
2 **TRUMP:** So, she's allowed to do that, but I'm not allowed
3 to respond?
4
5 Fact Checks of the Second Presidential Debate
6 Reporters for The New York Times fact-checked the
7 statements made by Hillary Clinton and Donald J. Trump
8 during Sunday's presidential debate.
9
10 **RADDATZ:** You're going to have — you're going to get to
11 respond right now.
12
13 **TRUMP:** Sounds fair.
14
15 **RADDATZ:** This tape is generating intense interest. In just
16 48 hours, it's become the single most talked about story of
17 the entire 2016 election on Facebook, with millions and
18 millions of people discussing it on the social network. As
19 we said a moment ago, we do want to bring in questions
20 from voters around country via social media, and our first
21 stays on this topic. Jeff from Ohio asks on Facebook,
22 "Trump says the campaign has changed him. When did
23 that happen?" So, Mr. Trump, let me add to that. When
24 you walked off that bus at age 59, were you a different
25 man or did that behavior continue until just recently? And
26 you have two minutes for this.
27
28 **TRUMP:** It was locker room talk, as I told you. That was
29 locker room talk. I'm not proud of it. I am a person who
30 has great respect for people, for my family, for the people
31 of this country. And certainly, I'm not proud of it. But that
32 was something that happened.
33

1 If you look at Bill Clinton, far worse. Mine are words, and
2 his was action. His was what he's done to women. There's
3 never been anybody in the history politics in this nation
4 that's been so abusive to women. So you can say any way
5 you want to say it, but Bill Clinton was abusive to women.
6
7 Hillary Clinton attacked those same women and attacked
8 them viciously. Four of them here tonight. One of the
9 women, who is a wonderful woman, at 12 years old, was
10 raped at 12. Her client she represented got him off, and
11 she's seen laughing on two separate occasions, laughing at
12 the girl who was raped. Kathy Shelton, that young woman
13 is here with us tonight.
14
15 So don't tell me about words. I am absolutely — I
16 apologize for those words. But it is things that people say.
17 But what President Clinton did, he was impeached, he lost
18 his license to practice law. He had to pay an $850,000 fine
19 to one of the women. Paula Jones, who's also here
20 tonight.
21
22 And I will tell you that when Hillary brings up a point like
23 that and she talks about words that I said 11 years ago, I
24 think it's disgraceful, and I think she should be ashamed of
25 herself, if you want to know the truth.
26
27   **(APPLAUSE)**
28
29 **RADDATZ:** Can we please hold the applause? Secretary
30 Clinton, you have two minutes.
31
32 **CLINTON:** Well, first, let me start by saying that so much of
33 what he's just said is not right, but he gets to run his
34 campaign any way he chooses. He gets to decide what he

84

1 wants to talk about. Instead of answering people's
2 questions, talking about our agenda, laying out the plans
3 that we have that we think can make a better life and a
4 better country, that's his choice.
5
6 When I hear something like that, I am reminded of what
7 my friend, Michelle Obama, advised us all: When they go
8 low, you go high.
9
10   **(APPLAUSE)**
11
12 And, look, if this were just about one video, maybe what
13 he's saying tonight would be understandable, but
14 everyone can draw their own conclusions at this point
15 about whether or not the man in the video or the man on
16 the stage respects women. But he never apologizes for
17 anything to anyone.
18
19 **CLINTON:** He never apologized to Mr. and Mrs. Khan, the
20 Gold Star family whose son, Captain Khan, died in the line
21 of duty in Iraq. And Donald insulted and attacked them for
22 weeks over their religion.
23
24 He never apologized to the distinguished federal judge
25 who was born in Indiana, but Donald said he couldn't be
26 trusted to be a judge because his parents were, quote,
27 "Mexican."
28
29 He never apologized to the reporter that he mimicked and
30 mocked on national television and our children were
31 watching. And he never apologized for the racist lie that
32 President Obama was not born in the United States of
33 America. He owes the president an apology, he owes our

1 country an apology, and he needs to take responsibility for
2 his actions and his words.
3
4 **TRUMP:** Well, you owe the president an apology, because
5 as you know very well, your campaign, Sidney Blumenthal
6 — he's another real winner that you have — and he's the
7 one that got this started, along with your campaign
8 manager, and they were on television just two weeks ago,
9 she was, saying exactly that. So you really owe him an
10 apology. You're the one that sent the pictures around your
11 campaign, sent the pictures around with President Obama
12 in a certain garb. That was long before I was ever involved,
13 so you actually owe an apology.
14
15 Number two, Michelle Obama. I've gotten to see the
16 commercials that they did on you. And I've gotten to see
17 some of the most vicious commercials I've ever seen of
18 Michelle Obama talking about you, Hillary.
19
20 So, you talk about friend? Go back and take a look at those
21 commercials, a race where you lost fair and square, unlike
22 the Bernie Sanders race, where you won, but not fair and
23 square, in my opinion. And all you have to do is take a look
24 at WikiLeaks and just see what they say about Bernie
25 Sanders and see what Deborah Wasserman Schultz had in
26 mind, because Bernie Sanders, between super-delegates
27 and Deborah Wasserman Schultz, he never had a chance.
28 And I was so surprised to see him sign on with the devil.
29
30 But when you talk about apology, I think the one that you
31 should really be apologizing for and the thing that you
32 should be apologizing for are the 33,000 e-mails that you
33 deleted, and that you acid washed, and then the two

1 boxes of e-mails and other things last week that were
2 taken from an office and are now missing.
3
4 And I'll tell you what. I didn't think I'd say this, but I'm
5 going to say it, and I hate to say it. But if I win, I am going
6 to instruct my attorney general to get a special prosecutor
7 to look into your situation, because there has never been
8 so many lies, so much deception. There has never been
9 anything like it, and we're going to have a special
10 prosecutor.
11
12 When I speak, I go out and speak, the people of this
13 country are furious. In my opinion, the people that have
14 been long-term workers at the FBI are furious. There has
15 never been anything like this, where e-mails — and you
16 get a subpoena, you get a subpoena, and after getting the
17 subpoena, you delete 33,000 e-mails, and then you acid
18 wash them or bleach them, as you would say, very
19 expensive process.
20
21 So we're going to get a special prosecutor, and we're going
22 to look into it, because you know what? People have been
23 — their lives have been destroyed for doing one-fifth of
24 what you've done. And it's a disgrace. And honestly, you
25 ought to be ashamed of yourself.
26
27 **RADDATZ:** Secretary Clinton, I want to follow up on that.
28
29 **(CROSSTALK)**
30
31 **RADDATZ:** I'm going to let you talk about e-mails.
32
33 **CLINTON:** ... because everything he just said is absolutely
34 false, but I'm not surprised.

1
2 **TRUMP:** Oh, really?
3
4 **CLINTON:** In the first debate...
5
6 **(LAUGHTER)**
7
8 **RADDATZ:** And really, the audience needs to calm down
9 here.
10
11 **CLINTON:** ... I told people that it would be impossible to be
12 fact-checking Donald all the time. I'd never get to talk
13 about anything I want to do and how we're going to really
14 make lives better for people.
15
16 So, once again, go to HillaryClinton.com. We have literally
17 Trump — you can fact check him in real time. Last time at
18 the first debate, we had millions of people fact checking,
19 so I expect we'll have millions more fact checking,
20 because, you know, it is — it's just awfully good that
21 someone with the temperament of Donald Trump is not in
22 charge of the law in our country.
23
24 **TRUMP:** Because you'd be in jail.
25
26 **(APPLAUSE)**
27
28 **RADDATZ:** Secretary Clinton...
29
30 **COOPER:** We want to remind the audience to please not
31 talk out loud. Please do not applaud. You're just wasting
32 time.
33

1 **RADDATZ:** And, Secretary Clinton, I do want to follow up
2 on e- mails. You've said your handing of your e-mails was a
3 mistake. You disagreed with FBI Director James Comey,
4 calling your handling of classified information, quote,
5 "extremely careless." The FBI said that there were 110
6 classified e-mails that were exchanged, eight of which
7 were top secret, and that it was possible hostile actors did
8 gain access to those e-mails. You don't call that extremely
9 careless?
10
11 **CLINTON:** Well, Martha, first, let me say — and I've said
12 before, but I'll repeat it, because I want everyone to hear
13 it — that was a mistake, and I take responsibility for using
14 a personal e-mail account. Obviously, if I were to do it over
15 again, I would not. I'm not making any excuses. It was a
16 mistake. And I am very sorry about that.
17
18 But I think it's also important to point out where there are
19 some misleading accusations from critics and others. After
20 a year-long investigation, there is no evidence that anyone
21 hacked the server I was using and there is no evidence that
22 anyone can point to at all — anyone who says otherwise
23 has no basis — that any classified material ended up in the
24 wrong hands.
25
26 I take classified materials very seriously and always have.
27 When I was on the Senate Armed Services Committee, I
28 was privy to a lot of classified material. Obviously, as
29 secretary of state, I had some of the most important
30 secrets that we possess, such as going after bin Laden. So I
31 am very committed to taking classified information
32 seriously. And as I said, there is no evidence that any
33 classified information ended up in the wrong hands.
34

1 **RADDATZ:** OK, we're going to move on.

2

3 **TRUMP:** And yet she didn't know the word — the letter C
4 on a document. Right? She didn't even know what that
5 word — what that letter meant.

6

7 You know, it's amazing. I'm watching Hillary go over facts.
8 And she's going after fact after fact, and she's lying again,
9 because she said she — you know, what she did with the
10 e-mail was fine. You think it was fine to delete 33,000 e-
11 mails? I don't think so.

12

13 She said the 33,000 e-mails had to do with her daughter's
14 wedding, number one, and a yoga class. Well, maybe we'll
15 give three or three or four or five or something. 33,000 e-
16 mails deleted, and now she's saying there wasn't anything
17 wrong.

18

19 And more importantly, that was after getting a subpoena.
20 That wasn't before. That was after. She got it from the
21 United States Congress. And I'll be honest, I am so
22 disappointed in congressmen, including Republicans, for
23 allowing this to happen.

24

25 Our Justice Department, where our husband goes on to
26 the back of a airplane for 39 minutes, talks to the attorney
27 general days before a ruling is going to be made on her
28 case. But for you to say that there was nothing wrong with
29 you deleting 39,000 e-mails, again, you should be ashamed
30 of yourself. What you did — and this is after getting a
31 subpoena from the United States Congress.

32

33 **COOPER:** We have to move on.

34

90

1 **TRUMP:** You did that. Wait a minute. One second.
2
3 **COOPER:** Secretary Clinton, you can respond, and then we
4 got to move on.
5
6 **RADDATZ:** We want to give the audience a chance.
7
8 **TRUMP:** If you did that in the private sector, you'd be put
9 in jail, let alone after getting a subpoena from the United
10 States Congress.
11
12 **COOPER:** Secretary Clinton, you can respond. Then we
13 have to move on to an audience question.
14
15 **CLINTON:** Look, it's just not true. And so please, go to...
16
17 **TRUMP:** Oh, you didn't delete them?
18
19 **COOPER:** Allow her to respond, please.
20
21 **CLINTON:** It was personal e-mails, not official.
22
23 **TRUMP:** Oh, 33,000? Yeah.
24
25 **CLINTON:** Not — well, we turned over 35,000, so...
26
27 **TRUMP:** Oh, yeah. What about the other 15,000?
28
29 **COOPER:** Please allow her to respond. She didn't talk while
30 you talked.
31
32 **CLINTON:** Yes, that's true, I didn't.
33
34 Trump and Clinton's Second Debate: Analysis

1 Here's how we analyzed in real time the second
2 presidential debate between Hillary Clinton and Donald J.
3 Trump.
4
5
6 **TRUMP:** Because you have nothing to say.
7
8 **CLINTON:** I didn't in the first debate, and I'm going to try
9 not to in this debate, because I'd like to get to the
10 questions that the people have brought here tonight to
11 talk to us about.
12
13 **TRUMP:** Get off this question.
14
15 **CLINTON:** OK, Donald. I know you're into big diversion
16 tonight, anything to avoid talking about your campaign
17 and the way it's exploding and the way Republicans are
18 leaving you. But let's at least focus...
19
20 **TRUMP:** Let's see what happens...
21
22   **(CROSSTALK)**
23
24 **COOPER:** Allow her to respond.
25
26 **CLINTON:** ... on some of the issues that people care about
27 tonight. Let's get to their questions.
28
29 **COOPER:** We have a question here from Ken Karpowicz.
30 He has a question about health care. Ken?
31
32 **TRUMP:** I'd like to know, Anderson, why aren't you
33 bringing up the e-mails? I'd like to know. Why aren't you
34 bringing...

1
2 **COOPER:** We brought up the e-mails.
3
4 **TRUMP:** No, it hasn't. It hasn't. And it hasn't been finished
5 at all.
6
7 **COOPER:** Ken Karpowicz has a question.
8
9 **TRUMP:** It's nice to — one on three.
10
11 **QUESTION:** Thank you. Affordable Care Act, known as
12 Obamacare, it is not affordable. Premiums have gone up.
13 Deductibles have gone up. Copays have gone up.
14 Prescriptions have gone up. And the coverage has gone
15 down. What will you do to bring the cost down and make
16 coverage better?
17
18 **COOPER:** That first one goes to Secretary Clinton, because
19 you started out the last one to the audience.
20
21 **CLINTON:** If he wants to start, he can start. No, go ahead,
22 Donald.
23
24 **TRUMP:** No, I'm a gentlemen, Hillary. Go ahead.
25
26 **(LAUGHTER)**
27
28 **COOPER:** Secretary Clinton?
29
30 **CLINTON:** Well, I think Donald was about to say he's going
31 to solve it by repealing it and getting rid of the Affordable
32 Care Act. And I'm going to fix it, because I agree with you.
33 Premiums have gotten too high. Copays, deductibles,

93

1   prescription drug costs, and I've laid out a series of actions
2   that we can take to try to get those costs down.
3

4   But here's what I don't want people to forget when we're
5   talking about reining in the costs, which has to be the
6   highest priority of the next president, when the Affordable
7   Care Act passed, it wasn't just that 20 million got
8   insurance who didn't have it before. But that in and of
9   itself was a good thing. I meet these people all the time,
10   and they tell me what a difference having that insurance
11   meant to them and their families.
12

13   But everybody else, the 170 million of us who get health
14   insurance through our employees got big benefits.
15   Number one, insurance companies can't deny you
16   coverage because of a pre-existing condition. Number two,
17   no lifetime limits, which is a big deal if you have serious
18   health problems.
19

20   Number three, women can't be charged more than men
21   for our health insurance, which is the way it used to be
22   before the Affordable Care Act. Number four, if you're
23   under 26, and your parents have a policy, you can be on
24   that policy until the age of 26, something that didn't
25   happen before.
26

27   So I want very much to save what works and is good about
28   the Affordable Care Act. But we've got to get costs down.
29   We've got to provide additional help to small businesses
30   so that they can afford to provide health insurance. But if
31   we repeal it, as Donald has proposed, and start over again,
32   all of those benefits I just mentioned are lost to
33   everybody, not just people who get their health insurance

1 on the exchange. And then we would have to start all over
2 again.
3
4 Right now, we are at 90 percent health insurance
5 coverage. That's the highest we've ever been in our
6 country.
7
8 **COOPER:** Secretary Clinton, your time is up.
9
10 **CLINTON:** So I want us to get to 100 percent, but get costs
11 down and keep quality up.
12
13 **COOPER:** Mr. Trump, you have two minutes.
14
15 **TRUMP:** It is such a great question and it's maybe the
16 question I get almost more than anything else, outside of
17 defense. Obamacare is a disaster. You know it. We all
18 know it. It's going up at numbers that nobody's ever seen
19 worldwide. Nobody's ever seen numbers like this for
20 health care.
21
22 It's only getting worse. In '17, it implodes by itself. Their
23 method of fixing it is to go back and ask Congress for more
24 money, more and more money. We have right now almost
25 $20 trillion in debt.
26
27 Obamacare will never work. It's very bad, very bad health
28 insurance. Far too expensive. And not only expensive for
29 the person that has it, unbelievably expensive for our
30 country. It's going to be one of the biggest line items very
31 shortly.
32
33 We have to repeal it and replace it with something
34 absolutely much less expensive and something that works,

1 where your plan can actually be tailored. We have to get
2 rid of the lines around the state, artificial lines, where we
3 stop insurance companies from coming in and competing,
4 because they want — and President Obama and whoever
5 was working on it — they want to leave those lines,
6 because that gives the insurance companies essentially
7 monopolies. We want competition.
8
9 You will have the finest health care plan there is. She
10 wants to go to a single-payer plan, which would be a
11 disaster, somewhat similar to Canada. And if you haven't
12 noticed the Canadians, when they need a big operation,
13 when something happens, they come into the United
14 States in many cases because their system is so slow. It's
15 catastrophic in certain ways.
16
17 But she wants to go to single payer, which means the
18 government basically rules everything. Hillary Clinton has
19 been after this for years. Obamacare was the first step.
20 Obamacare is a total disaster. And not only are your rates
21 going up by numbers that nobody's ever believed, but
22 your deductibles are going up, so that unless you get hit by
23 a truck, you're never going to be able to use it.
24
25 **COOPER:** Mr. Trump, your time...
26
27 **TRUMP:** It is a disastrous plan, and it has to be repealed
28 and replaced.
29
30 **COOPER:** Secretary Clinton, let me follow up with you.
31 Your husband called Obamacare, quote, "the craziest thing
32 in the world," saying that small-business owners are
33 getting killed as premiums double, coverage is cut in half.

1   Was he mistaken or was the mistake simply telling the
2   truth?
3
4   **CLINTON:** No, I mean, he clarified what he meant. And it's
5   very clear. Look, we are in a situation in our country where
6   if we were to start all over again, we might come up with a
7   different system. But we have an employer-based system.
8   That's where the vast majority of people get their health
9   care.
10
11   And the Affordable Care Act was meant to try to fill the
12   gap between people who were too poor and couldn't put
13   together any resources to afford health care, namely
14   people on Medicaid. Obviously, Medicare, which is a
15   single-payer system, which takes care of our elderly and
16   does a great job doing it, by the way, and then all of the
17   people who were employed, but people who were
18   working but didn't have the money to afford insurance
19   and didn't have anybody, an employer or anybody else, to
20   help them.
21
22   That was the slot that the Obamacare approach was to
23   take. And like I say, 20 million people now have health
24   insurance. So if we just rip it up and throw it away, what
25   Donald's not telling you is we just turn it back to the
26   insurance companies the way it used to be, and that
27   means the insurance companies...
28
29   **COOPER:** Secretary Clinton...
30
31   **CLINTON:** ... get to do pretty much whatever they want,
32   including saying, look, I'm sorry, you've got diabetes, you
33   had cancer, your child has asthma...
34

1　**COOPER:** Your time is up.

2

3　**CLINTON:** ... you may not be able to have insurance
4　because you can't afford it. So let's fix what's broken
5　about it, but let's not throw it away and give it all back to
6　the insurance companies and the drug companies. That's
7　not going to work.

8

9　**COOPER:** Mr. Trump, let me follow up on this. **TRUMP:**
10　Well, I just want — just one thing. First of all, Hillary,
11　everything's broken about it. Everything. Number two,
12　Bernie Sanders said that Hillary Clinton has very bad
13　judgment. This is a perfect example of it, trying to save
14　Obamacare, which is a disaster.

15

16　**COOPER:** You've said you want to end Obamacare...

17

18　**TRUMP:** By the way...

19

20　**COOPER:** You've said you want to end Obamacare. You've
21　also said you want to make coverage accessible for people
22　with pre-existing conditions. How do you force insurance
23　companies to do that if you're no longer mandating that
24　every American get insurance?

25

26　**TRUMP:** We're going to be able to. You're going to have
27　plans...

28

29　**COOPER:** What does that mean?

30

31　**TRUMP:** Well, I'll tell you what it means. You're going to
32　have plans that are so good, because we're going to have
33　so much competition in the insurance industry. Once we

1 break out — once we break out the lines and allow the
2 competition to come...
3
4 **COOPER:** Are you going — are you going to have a
5 mandate that Americans have to have health insurance?
6
7 **TRUMP:** President Obama — Anderson, excuse me.
8 President Obama, by keeping those lines, the boundary
9 lines around each state, it was almost gone until just very
10 toward the end of the passage of Obamacare, which, by
11 the way, was a fraud. You know that, because Jonathan
12 Gruber, the architect of Obamacare, was said — he said it
13 was a great lie, it was a big lie. President Obama said you
14 keep your doctor, you keep your plan. The whole thing
15 was a fraud, and it doesn't work.
16
17 But when we get rid of those lines, you will have
18 competition, and we will be able to keep pre-existing, we'll
19 also be able to help people that can't get — don't have
20 money because we are going to have people protected.
21
22 And Republicans feel this way, believe it or not, and
23 strongly this way. We're going to block grant into the
24 states. We're going to block grant into Medicaid into the
25 states...
26
27 **COOPER:** Thank you, Mr. Trump.
28
29 **TRUMP:** ... so that we will be able to take care of people
30 without the necessary funds to take care of themselves.
31
32 **COOPER:** Thank you, Mr. Trump.
33

1 **RADDATZ:** We now go to Gorbah Hamed with a question
2 for both candidates.
3
4 QUESTION: Hi. There are 3.3 million Muslims in the United
5 States, and I'm one of them. You've mentioned working
6 with Muslim nations, but with Islamophobia on the rise,
7 how will you help people like me deal with the
8 consequences of being labeled as a threat to the country
9 after the election is over?
10
11 **RADDATZ:** Mr. Trump, you're first.
12
13 **TRUMP:** Well, you're right about Islamophobia, and that's
14 a shame. But one thing we have to do is we have to make
15 sure that — because there is a problem. I mean, whether
16 we like it or not, and we could be very politically correct,
17 but whether we like it or not, there is a problem. And we
18 have to be sure that Muslims come in and report when
19 they see something going on. When they see hatred going
20 on, they have to report it.
21
22 As an example, in San Bernardino, many people saw the
23 bombs all over the apartment of the two people that killed
24 14 and wounded many, many people. Horribly wounded.
25 They'll never be the same. Muslims have to report the
26 problems when they see them.
27
28 And, you know, there's always a reason for everything. If
29 they don't do that, it's a very difficult situation for our
30 country, because you look at Orlando and you look at San
31 Bernardino and you look at the World Trade Center. Go
32 outside. Look at Paris. Look at that horrible — these are
33 radical Islamic terrorists.
34

1 And she won't even mention the word and nor will
2 President Obama. He won't use the term "radical Islamic
3 terrorism." Now, to solve a problem, you have to be able
4 to state what the problem is or at least say the name. She
5 won't say the name and President Obama won't say the
6 name. But the name is there. It's radical Islamic terror. And
7 before you solve it, you have to say the name.
8
9 **RADDATZ:** Secretary Clinton?
10
11 **CLINTON:** Well, thank you for asking your question. And
12 I've heard this question from a lot of Muslim-Americans
13 across our country, because, unfortunately, there's been a
14 lot of very divisive, dark things said about Muslims. And
15 even someone like Captain Khan, the young man who
16 sacrificed himself defending our country in the United
17 States Army, has been subject to attack by Donald.
18
19 I want to say just a couple of things. First, we've had
20 Muslims in America since George Washington. And we've
21 had many successful Muslims. We just lost a particular
22 well-known one with Muhammad Ali.
23
24 **CLINTON:** My vision of America is an America where
25 everyone has a place, if you're willing to work hard, you do
26 your part, you contribute to the community. That's what
27 America is. That's what we want America to be for our
28 children and our grandchildren.
29
30 It's also very short-sighted and even dangerous to be
31 engaging in the kind of demagogic rhetoric that Donald
32 has about Muslims. We need American Muslims to be part
33 of our eyes and ears on our front lines. I've worked with a
34 lot of different Muslim groups around America. I've met

1 with a lot of them, and I've heard how important it is for
2 them to feel that they are wanted and included and part of
3 our country, part of our homeland security, and that's
4 what I want to see.
5
6 It's also important I intend to defeat ISIS, to do so in a
7 coalition with majority Muslim nations. Right now, a lot of
8 those nations are hearing what Donald says and
9 wondering, why should we cooperate with the Americans?
10 And this is a gift to ISIS and the terrorists, violent jihadist
11 terrorists.
12
13 We are not at war with Islam. And it is a mistake and it
14 plays into the hands of the terrorists to act as though we
15 are. So I want a country where citizens like you and your
16 family are just as welcome as anyone else.
17
18 **RADDATZ:** Thank you, Secretary Clinton.
19
20 Mr. Trump, in December, you said this. "Donald J. Trump is
21 calling for a total and complete shutdown of Muslims
22 entering the United States until our country's
23 representatives can figure out what the hell is going on.
24 We have no choice. We have no choice." Your running
25 mate said this week that the Muslim ban is no longer your
26 position. Is that correct? And if it is, was it a mistake to
27 have a religious test?
28
29 **TRUMP:** First of all, Captain Khan is an American hero, and
30 if I were president at that time, he would be alive today,
31 because unlike her, who voted for the war without
32 knowing what she was doing, I would not have had our
33 people in Iraq. Iraq was disaster. So he would have been
34 alive today.

1
2 The Muslim ban is something that in some form has
3 morphed into a extreme vetting from certain areas of the
4 world. Hillary Clinton wants to allow hundreds of
5 thousands — excuse me. Excuse me..
6
7 **RADDATZ:** And why did it morph into that? No, did you —
8 no, answer the question. Do you still believe...
9
10 **TRUMP:** Why don't you interrupt her? You interrupt me all
11 the time.
12
13 **RADDATZ:** I do.
14
15 **TRUMP:** Why don't you interrupt her?
16
17 **RADDATZ:** Would you please explain whether or not the
18 Muslim ban still stands?
19
20 **TRUMP:** It's called extreme vetting. We are going to areas
21 like Syria where they're coming in by the tens of
22 thousands because of Barack Obama. And Hillary Clinton
23 wants to allow a 550 percent increase over Obama. People
24 are coming into our country like we have no idea who they
25 are, where they are from, what their feelings about our
26 country is, and she wants 550 percent more. This is going
27 to be the great Trojan horse of all time.
28
29 We have enough problems in this country. I believe in
30 building safe zones. I believe in having other people pay
31 for them, as an example, the Gulf states, who are not
32 carrying their weight, but they have nothing but money,
33 and take care of people. But I don't want to have, with all
34 the problems this country has and all of the problems that

1 you see going on, hundreds of thousands of people coming
2 in from Syria when we know nothing about them. We
3 know nothing about their values and we know nothing
4 about their love for our country.
5
6 **RADDATZ:** And, Secretary Clinton, let me ask you about
7 that, because you have asked for an increase from 10,000
8 to 65,000 Syrian refugees. We know you want tougher
9 vetting. That's not a perfect system. So why take the risk
10 of having those refugees come into the country?
11
12 **CLINTON:** Well, first of all, I will not let anyone into our
13 country that I think poses a risk to us. But there are a lot of
14 refugees, women and children — think of that picture we
15 all saw of that 4-year-old boy with the blood on his
16 forehead because he'd been bombed by the Russian and
17 Syrian air forces.
18
19 There are children suffering in this catastrophic war,
20 largely, I believe, because of Russian aggression. And we
21 need to do our part. We by no means are carrying
22 anywhere near the load that Europe and others are. But
23 we will have vetting that is as tough as it needs to be from
24 our professionals, our intelligence experts and others.
25
26 But it is important for us as a policy, you know, not to say,
27 as Donald has said, we're going to ban people based on a
28 religion. How do you do that? We are a country founded
29 on religious freedom and liberty. How do we do what he
30 has advocated without causing great distress within our
31 own county? Are we going to have religious tests when
32 people fly into our country? And how do we expect to be
33 able to implement those?
34

1 So I thought that what he said was extremely unwise and
2 even dangerous. And indeed, you can look at the
3 propaganda on a lot of the terrorists sites, and what
4 Donald Trump says about Muslims is used to recruit
5 fighters, because they want to create a war between us.
6
7 And the final thing I would say, this is the 10th or 12th
8 time that he's denied being for the war in Iraq. We have it
9 on tape. The entire press corps has looked at it. It's been
10 debunked, but it never stops him from saying whatever he
11 wants to say.
12
13 **TRUMP:** That's not been debunked.
14
15 **CLINTON:** So, please...
16
17 **TRUMP:** That has not been debunked.
18
19 **CLINTON:** ... go to HillaryClinton.com and you can see it.
20
21 **TRUMP:** I was against — I was against the war in Iraq. Has
22 not been debunked. And you voted for it. And you
23 shouldn't have. Well, I just want to say...
24
25 **RADDATZ:** There's been lots of fact-checking on that. I'd
26 like to move on to an online question...
27
28 **TRUMP:** Excuse me. She just went about 25 seconds over
29 her time.
30
31 **RADDATZ:** She did not.
32
33 **TRUMP:** Could I just respond to this, please?
34

1 **RADDATZ:** Very quickly, please.

2

3 **TRUMP:** Hillary Clinton, in terms of having people come
4 into our country, we have many criminal illegal aliens.
5 When we want to send them back to their country, their
6 country says we don't want them. In some cases, they're
7 murderers, drug lords, drug problems. And they don't
8 want them.

9

10 And Hillary Clinton, when she was secretary of state, said
11 that's OK, we can't force it into their country. Let me tell
12 you, I'm going to force them right back into their country.
13 They're murderers and some very bad people.

14

15 And I will tell you very strongly, when Bernie Sanders said
16 she had bad judgment, she has really bad judgment,
17 because we are letting people into this country that are
18 going to cause problems and crime like you've never seen.
19 We're also letting drugs pour through our southern border
20 at a record clip. At a record clip. And it shouldn't be
21 allowed to happen.

22

23 ICE just endorsed me. They've never endorsed a
24 presidential candidate. The Border Patrol agents, 16,500,
25 just recently endorsed me, and they endorsed me because
26 I understand the border. She doesn't. She wants amnesty
27 for everybody. Come right in. Come right over. It's a
28 horrible thing she's doing. She's got bad judgment, and
29 honestly, so bad that she should never be president of the
30 United States. That I can tell you.

31

32 **RADDATZ:** Thank you, Mr. Trump. I want to move on. This
33 next question from the public through the Bipartisan Open
34 Debate Coalition's online forum, where Americans

106

1 submitted questions that generated millions of votes. This
2 question involves WikiLeaks release of purported excerpts
3 of Secretary Clinton's paid speeches, which she has
4 refused to release, and one line in particular, in which you,
5 Secretary Clinton, purportedly say you need both a public
6 and private position on certain issues. So, Tu (ph), from
7 Virginia asks, is it OK for politicians to be two-faced? Is it
8 acceptable for a politician to have a private stance on
9 issues? Secretary Clinton, your two minutes.
10
11 **CLINTON:** Well, right. As I recall, that was something I said
12 about Abraham Lincoln after having seen the wonderful
13 Steven Spielberg movie called "Lincoln." It was a master
14 class watching President Lincoln get the Congress to
15 approve the 13th Amendment. It was principled, and it
16 was strategic.
17
18 And I was making the point that it is hard sometimes to
19 get the Congress to do what you want to do and you have
20 to keep working at it. And, yes, President Lincoln was
21 trying to convince some people, he used some arguments,
22 convincing other people, he used other arguments. That
23 was a great — I thought a great display of presidential
24 leadership.
25
26 But, you know, let's talk about what's really going on here,
27 Martha, because our intelligence community just came out
28 and said in the last few days that the Kremlin, meaning
29 Putin and the Russian government, are directing the
30 attacks, the hacking on American accounts to influence
31 our election. And WikiLeaks is part of that, as are other
32 sites where the Russians hack information, we don't even
33 know if it's accurate information, and then they put it out.
34

1   We have never in the history of our country been in a
2   situation where an adversary, a foreign power, is working
3   so hard to influence the outcome of the election. And
4   believe me, they're not doing it to get me elected. They're
5   doing it to try to influence the election for Donald Trump.
6
7   **CLINTON:** Now, maybe because he has praised Putin,
8   maybe because he says he agrees with a lot of what Putin
9   wants to do, maybe because he wants to do business in
10   Moscow, I don't know the reasons. But we deserve
11   answers. And we should demand that Donald release all of
12   his tax returns so that people can see what are the
13   entanglements and the financial relationships that he
14   has...
15
16   **RADDATZ:** We're going to get to that later. Secretary
17   Clinton, you're out of time.
18
19   **CLINTON:** ... with the Russians and other foreign powers.
20
21   **RADDATZ:** Mr. Trump?
22
23   **TRUMP:** Well, I think I should respond, because — so
24   ridiculous. Look, now she's blaming — she got caught in a
25   total lie. Her papers went out to all her friends at the
26   banks, Goldman Sachs and everybody else, and she said
27   things — WikiLeaks that just came out. And she lied. Now
28   she's blaming the lie on the late, great Abraham Lincoln.
29   That's one that I haven't...
30
31   (LAUGHTER)
32
33   OK, Honest Abe, Honest Abe never lied. That's the good
34   thing. That's the big difference between Abraham Lincoln

1 and you. That's a big, big difference. We're talking about
2 some difference.
3
4 But as far as other elements of what she was saying, I
5 don't know Putin. I think it would be great if we got along
6 with Russia because we could fight ISIS together, as an
7 example. But I don't know Putin.
8
9 But I notice, anytime anything wrong happens, they like to
10 say the Russians are — she doesn't know if it's the
11 Russians doing the hacking. Maybe there is no hacking. But
12 they always blame Russia. And the reason they blame
13 Russia because they think they're trying to tarnish me with
14 Russia. I know nothing about Russia. I know — I know
15 about Russia, but I know nothing about the inner workings
16 of Russia. I don't deal there. I have no businesses there. I
17 have no loans from Russia.
18
19 I have a very, very great balance sheet, so great that when
20 I did the Old Post Office on Pennsylvania Avenue, the
21 United States government, because of my balance sheet,
22 which they actually know very well, chose me to do the
23 Old Post Office, between the White House and Congress,
24 chose me to do the Old Post Office. One of the primary
25 area things, in fact, perhaps the primary thing was balance
26 sheet. But I have no loans with Russia. You could go to the
27 United States government, and they would probably tell
28 you that, because they know my sheet very well in order
29 to get that development I had to have.
30
31 Now, the taxes are a very simple thing. As soon as I have
32 — first of all, I pay hundreds of millions of dollars in taxes.
33 Many of her friends took bigger deductions. Warren
34 Buffett took a massive deduction. Soros, who's a friend of

1 hers, took a massive deduction. Many of the people that
2 are giving her all this money that she can do many more
3 commercials than me gave her — took massive
4 deductions.
5
6 I pay hundreds of millions of dollars in taxes. But — but as
7 soon as my routine audit is finished, I'll release my returns.
8 I'll be very proud to. They're actually quite great.
9
10 **RADDATZ:** Thank you, Mr. Trump.
11
12 **COOPER:** We want to turn, actually, to the topic of taxes.
13 We have a question from Spencer Maass. Spencer?
14
15 **QUESTION:** Good evening. My question is, what specific
16 tax provisions will you change to ensure the wealthiest
17 Americans pay their fair share in taxes?
18
19 **COOPER:** Mr. Trump, you have two minutes.
20
21 **TRUMP:** Well, one thing I'd do is get rid of carried interest.
22 One of the greatest provisions for people like me, to be
23 honest with you, I give up a lot when I run, because I knock
24 out the tax code. And she could have done this years ago,
25 by the way. She's a United States — she was a United
26 States senator.
27
28 She complains that Donald Trump took advantage of the
29 tax code. Well, why didn't she change it? Why didn't you
30 change it when you were a senator? The reason you didn't
31 is that all your friends take the same advantage that I do.
32 And I do. You have provisions in the tax code that, frankly,
33 we could change. But you wouldn't change it, because all

1 of these people gave you the money so you can take
2 negative ads on Donald Trump.
3
4 But — and I say that about a lot of things. You know, I've
5 heard Hillary complaining about so many different things
6 over the years. "I wish you would have done this." But
7 she's been there for 30 years she's been doing this stuff.
8 She never changed. And she never will change. She never
9 will change.
10
11 We're getting rid of carried interest provisions. I'm
12 lowering taxes actually, because I think it's so important
13 for corporations, because we have corporations leaving —
14 massive corporations and little ones, little ones can't form.
15 We're getting rid of regulations which goes hand in hand
16 with the lowering of the taxes.
17
18 But we're bringing the tax rate down from 35 percent to
19 15 percent. We're cutting taxes for the middle class. And I
20 will tell you, we are cutting them big league for the middle
21 class.
22
23 And I will tell you, Hillary Clinton is raising your taxes,
24 folks. You can look at me. She's raising your taxes really
25 high. And what that's going to do is a disaster for the
26 country. But she is raising your taxes and I'm lowering your
27 taxes. That in itself is a big difference. We are going to be
28 thriving again. We have no growth in this country. There's
29 no growth. If China has a GDP of 7 percent, it's like a
30 national catastrophe. We're down at 1 percent. And that's,
31 like, no growth. And we're going lower, in my opinion. And
32 a lot of it has to do with the fact that our taxes are so high,
33 just about the highest in the world. And I'm bringing them
34 down to one of the lower in the world. And I think it's so

1 important — one of the most important things we can do.
2 But she is raising everybody's taxes massively.
3
4 **COOPER:** Secretary Clinton, you have two minutes. The
5 question was, what specific tax provisions will you change
6 to ensure the wealthiest Americans pay their fair share of
7 taxes?
8
9 **CLINTON:** Well, everything you've heard just now from
10 Donald is not true. I'm sorry I have to keep saying this, but
11 he lives in an alternative reality. And it is sort of amusing
12 to hear somebody who hasn't paid federal income taxes in
13 maybe 20 years talking about what he's going to do.
14
15 But I'll tell you what he's going to do. His plan will give the
16 wealthy and corporations the biggest tax cuts they've ever
17 had, more than the Bush tax cuts by at least a factor of
18 two. Donald always takes care of Donald and people like
19 Donald, and this would be a massive gift. And, indeed, the
20 way that he talks about his tax cuts would end up raising
21 taxes on middle-class families, millions of middle-class
22 families.
23
24 Now, here's what I want to do. I have said nobody who
25 makes less than $250,000 a year — and that's the vast
26 majority of Americans as you know — will have their taxes
27 raised, because I think we've got to go where the money
28 is. And the money is with people who have taken
29 advantage of every single break in the tax code.
30
31 And, yes, when I was a senator, I did vote to close
32 corporate loopholes. I voted to close, I think, one of the
33 loopholes he took advantage of when he claimed a billion-
34 dollar loss that enabled him to avoid paying taxes.

1
2 I want to have a tax on people who are making a million
3 dollars. It's called the Buffett rule. Yes, Warren Buffett is
4 the one who's gone out and said somebody like him
5 should not be paying a lower tax rate than his secretary. I
6 want to have a surcharge on incomes above $5 million.
7
8 We have to make up for lost times, because I want to
9 invest in you. I want to invest in hard-working families.
10 And I think it's been unfortunate, but it's happened, that
11 since the Great Recession, the gains have all gone to the
12 top. And we need to reverse that.
13
14 People like Donald, who paid zero in taxes, zero for our
15 vets, zero for our military, zero for health and education,
16 that is wrong.
17
18 **COOPER:** Thank you, Secretary.
19
20 **CLINTON:** And we're going to make sure that nobody, no
21 corporation, and no individual can get away without
22 paying his fair share to support our country.
23
24 **COOPER:** Thank you. I want to give you — Mr. Trump, I
25 want to give you the chance to respond. I just wanted to
26 tell our viewers what she's referring to. In the last month,
27 taxes were the number-one issue on Facebook for the first
28 time in the campaign. The New York Times published three
29 pages of your 1995 tax returns. They show you claimed a
30 $916 million loss, which means you could have avoided
31 paying personal federal income taxes for years. You've
32 said you pay state taxes, employee taxes, real estate taxes,
33 property taxes. You have not answered, though, a simple

1 question. Did you use that $916 million loss to avoid
2 paying personal federal income taxes for years?

3

4 **TRUMP:** Of course I do. Of course I do. And so do all of her
5 donors, or most of her donors. I know many of her donors.
6 Her donors took massive tax write-offs.

7

8 **COOPER:** So have you (inaudible) personal federal income
9 tax?

10

11 **TRUMP:** A lot of my — excuse me, Anderson — a lot of my
12 write- off was depreciation and other things that Hillary as
13 a senator allowed. And she'll always allow it, because the
14 people that give her all this money, they want it. That's
15 why.

16

17 See, I understand the tax code better than anybody that's
18 ever run for president. Hillary Clinton — and it's extremely
19 complex — Hillary Clinton has friends that want all of
20 these provisions, including they want the carried interest
21 provision, which is very important to Wall Street people.
22 But they really want the carried interest provision, which I
23 believe Hillary's leaving. Very interesting why she's leaving
24 carried interest.

25

26 But I will tell you that, number one, I pay tremendous
27 numbers of taxes. I absolutely used it. And so did Warren
28 Buffett and so did George Soros and so did many of the
29 other people that Hillary is getting money from. Now, I
30 won't mention their names, because they're rich, but
31 they're not famous. So we won't make them famous.

32

33 **COOPER:** So can you — can you say how many years you
34 have avoided paying personal federal income taxes?

114

1
2 **TRUMP:** No, but I pay tax, and I pay federal tax, too. But I
3 have a write-off, a lot of it's depreciation, which is a
4 wonderful charge. I love depreciation. You know, she's
5 given it to us.
6
7 Hey, if she had a problem — for 30 years she's been doing
8 this, Anderson. I say it all the time. She talks about health
9 care. Why didn't she do something about it? She talks
10 about taxes. Why didn't she do something about it? She
11 doesn't do anything about anything other than talk. With
12 her, it's all talk and no action.
13
14 **COOPER:** In the past...
15
16 **TRUMP:** And, again, Bernie Sanders, it's really bad
17 judgment. She has made bad judgment not only on taxes.
18 She's made bad judgments on Libya, on Syria, on Iraq. I
19 mean, her and Obama, whether you like it or not, the way
20 they got out of Iraq, the vacuum they've left, that's why
21 ISIS formed in the first place. They started from that little
22 area, and now they're in 32 different nations, Hillary.
23 Congratulations. Great job.
24
25 **COOPER:** Secretary — I want you to be able to respond,
26 Secretary Clinton.
27
28 **CLINTON:** Well, here we go again. I've been in favor of
29 getting rid of carried interest for years, starting when I was
30 a senator from New York. But that's not the point here.
31
32 **TRUMP:** Why didn't you do it? Why didn't you do it?
33
34 **COOPER:** Allow her to respond.

1

2 **CLINTON:** Because I was a senator with a Republican
3 president.

4

5 **TRUMP:** Oh, really?

6

7 **CLINTON:** I will be the president and we will get it done.
8 That's exactly right.

9

10 **TRUMP:** You could have done it, if you were an effective
11 — if you were an effective senator, you could have done it.
12 If you were an effective senator, you could have done it.
13 But you were not an effective senator.

14

15 **COOPER:** Please allow her to respond. She didn't interrupt
16 you.

17

18 **CLINTON:** You know, under our Constitution, presidents
19 have something called veto power. Look, he has now said
20 repeatedly, "30 years this and 30 years that." So let me
21 talk about my 30 years in public service. I'm very glad to
22 do so.

23

24 Eight million kids every year have health insurance,
25 because when I was first lady I worked with Democrats
26 and Republicans to create the Children's Health Insurance
27 Program. Hundreds of thousands of kids now have a
28 chance to be adopted because I worked to change our
29 adoption and foster care system. After 9/11, I went to
30 work with Republican mayor, governor and president to
31 rebuild New York and to get health care for our first
32 responders who were suffering because they had run
33 toward danger and gotten sickened by it. Hundreds of
34 thousands of National Guard and Reserve members have

1 health care because of work that I did, and children have
2 safer medicines because I was able to pass a law that
3 required the dosing to be more carefully done.
4
5 When I was secretary of state, I went around the world
6 advocating for our country, but also advocating for
7 women's rights, to make sure that women had a decent
8 chance to have a better life and negotiated a treaty with
9 Russia to lower nuclear weapons. Four hundred pieces of
10 legislation have my name on it as a sponsor or cosponsor
11 when I was a senator for eight years.
12
13
14 I worked very hard and was very proud to be re-elected in
15 New York by an even bigger margin than I had been
16 elected the first time. And as president, I will take that
17 work, that bipartisan work, that finding common ground,
18 because you have to be able to get along with people to
19 get things done in Washington.
20
21 **COOPER:** Thank you, secretary.
22
23 **CLINTON:** I've proven that I can, and for 30 years, I've
24 produced results for people.
25
26 **COOPER:** Thank you, secretary.
27
28 **RADDATZ:** We're going to move on to Syria. Both of you
29 have mentioned that.
30
31 **TRUMP:** She said a lot of things that were false. I mean, I
32 think we should be allowed to maybe...
33

1 **RADDATZ:** No, we can — no, Mr. Trump, we're going to go
2 on. This is about the audience.
3
4 **TRUMP:** Excuse me. Because she has been a disaster as a
5 senator. A disaster.
6
7 **RADDATZ:** Mr. Trump, we're going to move on. The heart-
8 breaking video of a 5-year-old Syrian boy named Omran
9 sitting in an ambulance after being pulled from the rubble
10 after an air strike in Aleppo focused the world's attention
11 on the horrors of the war in Syria, with 136 million views
12 on Facebook alone.
13
14 But there are much worse images coming out of Aleppo
15 every day now, where in the past few weeks alone, 400
16 people have been killed, at least 100 of them children. Just
17 days ago, the State Department called for a war crimes
18 investigation of the Syrian regime of Bashar al-Assad and
19 its ally, Russia, for their bombardment of Aleppo.
20
21 So this next question comes through social media through
22 Facebook. Diane from Pennsylvania asks, if you were
23 president, what would you do about Syria and the
24 humanitarian crisis in Aleppo? Isn't it a lot like the
25 Holocaust when the U.S. waited too long before we
26 helped? Secretary Clinton, we will begin with your two
27 minutes.
28
29 **CLINTON:** Well, the situation in Syria is catastrophic. And
30 every day that goes by, we see the results of the regime by
31 Assad in partnership with the Iranians on the ground, the
32 Russians in the air, bombarding places, in particular
33 Aleppo, where there are hundreds of thousands of people,
34 probably about 250,000 still left. And there is a

1 determined effort by the Russian air force to destroy
2 Aleppo in order to eliminate the last of the Syrian rebels
3 who are really holding out against the Assad regime.
4
5 Russia hasn't paid any attention to ISIS. They're interested
6 in keeping Assad in power. So I, when I was secretary of
7 state, advocated and I advocate today a no-fly zone and
8 safe zones. We need some leverage with the Russians,
9 because they are not going to come to the negotiating
10 table for a diplomatic resolution, unless there is some
11 leverage over them. And we have to work more closely
12 with our partners and allies on the ground.
13
14 But I want to emphasize that what is at stake here is the
15 ambitions and the aggressiveness of Russia. Russia has
16 decided that it's all in, in Syria. And they've also decided
17 who they want to see become president of the United
18 States, too, and it's not me. I've stood up to Russia. I've
19 taken on Putin and others, and I would do that as
20 president.
21
22 I think wherever we can cooperate with Russia, that's fine.
23 And I did as secretary of state. That's how we got a treaty
24 reducing nuclear weapons. It's how we got the sanctions
25 on Iran that put a lid on the Iranian nuclear program
26 without firing a single shot. So I would go to the
27 negotiating table with more leverage than we have now.
28 But I do support the effort to investigate for crimes, war
29 crimes committed by the Syrians and the Russians and try
30 to hold them accountable.
31
32 **RADDATZ:** Thank you, Secretary Clinton. Mr. Trump?
33

1 **TRUMP:** First of all, she was there as secretary of state
2 with the so-called line in the sand, which...
3
4 **CLINTON:** No, I wasn't. I was gone. I hate to interrupt you,
5 but at some point...
6
7 **TRUMP:** OK. But you were in contact — excuse me. You
8 were...
9
10 **CLINTON:** At some point, we need to do some fact-
11 checking here.
12
13 **TRUMP:** You were in total contact with the White House,
14 and perhaps, sadly, Obama probably still listened to you. I
15 don't think he would be listening to you very much
16 anymore.
17
18 Obama draws the line in the sand. It was laughed at all
19 over the world what happened.
20
21 Now, with that being said, she talks tough against Russia.
22 But our nuclear program has fallen way behind, and
23 they've gone wild with their nuclear program. Not good.
24 Our government shouldn't have allowed that to happen.
25 Russia is new in terms of nuclear. We are old. We're tired.
26 We're exhausted in terms of nuclear. A very bad thing.
27
28 Now, she talks tough, she talks really tough against Putin
29 and against Assad. She talks in favor of the rebels. She
30 doesn't even know who the rebels are. You know, every
31 time we take rebels, whether it's in Iraq or anywhere else,
32 we're arming people. And you know what happens? They
33 end up being worse than the people.
34

1 Look at what she did in Libya with Gadhafi. Gadhafi's out.
2 It's a mess. And, by the way, ISIS has a good chunk of their
3 oil. I'm sure you probably have heard that. It was a
4 disaster. Because the fact is, almost everything she's done
5 in foreign policy has been a mistake and it's been a
6 disaster.
7
8 But if you look at Russia, just take a look at Russia, and
9 look at what they did this week, where I agree, she wasn't
10 there, but possibly she's consulted. We sign a peace
11 treaty. Everyone's all excited. Well, what Russia did with
12 Assad and, by the way, with Iran, who you made very
13 powerful with the dumbest deal perhaps I've ever seen in
14 the history of deal-making, the Iran deal, with the $150
15 billion, with the $1.7 billion in cash, which is enough to fill
16 up this room.
17
18 But look at that deal. Iran now and Russia are now against
19 us. So she wants to fight. She wants to fight for rebels.
20 There's only one problem. You don't even know who the
21 rebels are. So what's the purpose?
22
23 **RADDATZ:** Mr. Trump, Mr. Trump, your two minutes is up.
24
25 **TRUMP:** And one thing I have to say.
26
27 **RADDATZ:** Your two minutes is up.
28
29 **TRUMP:** I don't like Assad at all, but Assad is killing ISIS.
30 Russia is killing ISIS. And Iran is killing ISIS. And those three
31 have now lined up because of our weak foreign policy.
32
33 **RADDATZ:** Mr. Trump, let me repeat the question. If you
34 were president...

1
2   **(LAUGHTER)**
3
4 ... what would you do about Syria and the humanitarian
5 crisis in Aleppo? And I want to remind you what your
6 running mate said. He said provocations by Russia need to
7 be met with American strength and that if Russia
8 continues to be involved in air strikes along with the Syrian
9 government forces of Assad, the United States of America
10 should be prepared to use military force to strike the
11 military targets of the Assad regime.
12
13 **TRUMP:** OK. He and I haven't spoken, and I disagree. I
14 disagree.
15
16 **RADDATZ:** You disagree with your running mate?
17
18 **TRUMP:** I think you have to knock out ISIS. Right now,
19 Syria is fighting ISIS. We have people that want to fight
20 both at the same time. But Syria is no longer Syria. Syria is
21 Russia and it's Iran, who she made strong and Kerry and
22 Obama made into a very powerful nation and a very rich
23 nation, very, very quickly, very, very quickly.
24
25 I believe we have to get ISIS. We have to worry about ISIS
26 before we can get too much more involved. She had a
27 chance to do something with Syria. They had a chance.
28 And that was the line. And she didn't.
29
30 **RADDATZ:** What do you think will happen if Aleppo falls?
31
32 **TRUMP:** I think Aleppo is a disaster, humanitarian-wise.
33
34 **RADDATZ:** What do you think will happen if it falls?

1
2 **TRUMP:** I think that it basically has fallen. OK? It basically
3 has fallen. Let me tell you something. You take a look at
4 Mosul. The biggest problem I have with the stupidity of
5 our foreign policy, we have Mosul. They think a lot of the
6 ISIS leaders are in Mosul. So we have announcements
7 coming out of Washington and coming out of Iraq, we will
8 be attacking Mosul in three weeks or four weeks.
9
10 Well, all of these bad leaders from ISIS are leaving Mosul.
11 Why can't they do it quietly? Why can't they do the attack,
12 make it a sneak attack, and after the attack is made,
13 inform the American public that we've knocked out the
14 leaders, we've had a tremendous success? People leave.
15 Why do they have to say we're going to be attacking
16 Mosul within the next four to six weeks, which is what
17 they're saying? How stupid is our country? **RADDATZ:**
18 There are sometimes reasons the military does that.
19 Psychological warfare.
20
21 **TRUMP:** I can't think of any. I can't think of any. And I'm
22 pretty good at it.
23
24 **RADDATZ:** It might be to help get civilians out.
25
26 **TRUMP:** And we have General Flynn. And we have — look,
27 I have 200 generals and admirals who endorsed me. I have
28 21 Congressional Medal of Honor recipients who endorsed
29 me. We talk about it all the time. They understand, why
30 can't they do something secretively, where they go in and
31 they knock out the leadership? How — why would these
32 people stay there? I've been reading now...
33
34 **RADDATZ:** Tell me what your strategy is.

1
2 **TRUMP:** ... for weeks — I've been reading now for weeks
3 about Mosul, that it's the harbor of where — you know,
4 between Raqqa and Mosul, this is where they think the
5 ISIS leaders are. Why would they be saying — they're not
6 staying there anymore. They're gone. Because everybody's
7 talking about how Iraq, which is us with our leadership,
8 goes in to fight Mosul.
9
10 Now, with these 200 admirals and generals, they can't
11 believe it. All I say is this. General George Patton, General
12 Douglas MacArthur are spinning in their grave at the
13 stupidity of what we're doing in the Middle East.
14
15 **RADDATZ:** I'm going to go to Secretary Clinton. Secretary
16 Clinton, you want Assad to go. You advocated arming
17 rebels, but it looks like that may be too late for Aleppo.
18 You talk about diplomatic efforts. Those have failed.
19 Cease-fires have failed. Would you introduce the threat of
20 U.S. military force beyond a no-fly zone against the Assad
21 regime to back up diplomacy?
22
23 **CLINTON:** I would not use American ground forces in Syria.
24 I think that would be a very serious mistake. I don't think
25 American troops should be holding territory, which is what
26 they would have to do as an occupying force. I don't think
27 that is a smart strategy.
28
29 I do think the use of special forces, which we're using, the
30 use of enablers and trainers in Iraq, which has had some
31 positive effects, are very much in our interests, and so I do
32 support what is happening, but let me just...
33

1 **RADDATZ:** But what would you do differently than
2 President Obama is doing?

3

4 **CLINTON:** Well, Martha, I hope that by the time I — if I'm
5 fortunate...

6

7 **TRUMP:** Everything.

8

9 **CLINTON:** I hope by the time I am president that we will
10 have pushed ISIS out of Iraq. I do think that there is a good
11 chance that we can take Mosul. And, you know, Donald
12 says he knows more about ISIS than the generals. No, he
13 doesn't.

14

15 There are a lot of very important planning going on, and
16 some of it is to signal to the Sunnis in the area, as well as
17 Kurdish Peshmerga fighters, that we all need to be in this.
18 And that takes a lot of planning and preparation.

19

20 I would go after Baghdadi. I would specifically target
21 Baghdadi, because I think our targeting of Al Qaida leaders
22 — and I was involved in a lot of those operations, highly
23 classified ones — made a difference. So I think that could
24 help.

25

26 I would also consider arming the Kurds. The Kurds have
27 been our best partners in Syria, as well as Iraq. And I know
28 there's a lot of concern about that in some circles, but I
29 think they should have the equipment they need so that
30 Kurdish and Arab fighters on the ground are the principal
31 way that we take Raqqa after pushing ISIS out of Iraq.

32

33 **RADDATZ:** Thank you very much. We're going to move
34 on...

125

1

2 **TRUMP:** You know what's funny? She went over a minute
3 over, and you don't stop her. When I go one second over,
4 it's like a big deal.

5

6 **RADDATZ:** You had many answers.

7

8 **TRUMP:** It's really — it's really very interesting.

9

10 **COOPER:** We've got a question over here from James
11 Carter. Mr. Carter?

12

13 **QUESTION:** My question is, do you believe you can be a
14 devoted president to all the people in the United States?

15

16 **COOPER:** That question begins for Mr. Trump.

17

18 **TRUMP:** Absolutely. I mean, she calls our people
19 deplorable, a large group, and irredeemable. I will be a
20 president for all of our people. And I'll be a president that
21 will turn our inner cities around and will give strength to
22 people and will give economics to people and will bring
23 jobs back.

24

25 Because NAFTA, signed by her husband, is perhaps the
26 greatest disaster trade deal in the history of the world. Not
27 in this country. It stripped us of manufacturing jobs. We
28 lost our jobs. We lost our money. We lost our plants. It is a
29 disaster. And now she wants to sign TPP, even though she
30 says now she's for it. She called it the gold standard. And
31 by the way, at the last debate, she lied, because it turned
32 out that she did say the gold standard and she said she
33 didn't say it. They actually said that she lied. OK? And she
34 lied. But she's lied about a lot of things.

1
2 **TRUMP:** I would be a president for all of the people,
3 African- Americans, the inner cities. Devastating what's
4 happening to our inner cities. She's been talking about it
5 for years. As usual, she talks about it, nothing happens.
6 She doesn't get it done.
7
8 Same with the Latino Americans, the Hispanic Americans.
9 The same exact thing. They talk, they don't get it done.
10 You go into the inner cities and — you see it's 45 percent
11 poverty. African- Americans now 45 percent poverty in the
12 inner cities. The education is a disaster. Jobs are essentially
13 nonexistent.
14
15 I mean, it's — you know, and I've been saying at big
16 speeches where I have 20,000 and 30,000 people, what do
17 you have to lose? It can't get any worse. And she's been
18 talking about the inner cities for 25 years. Nothing's going
19 to ever happen.
20
21 Let me tell you, if she's president of the United States,
22 nothing's going to happen. It's just going to be talk. And all
23 of her friends, the taxes we were talking about, and I
24 would just get it by osmosis. She's not doing any me
25 favors. But by doing all the others' favors, she's doing me
26 favors.
27
28 **COOPER:** Mr. Trump, thank you.
29
30 **TRUMP:** But I will tell you, she's all talk. It doesn't get
31 done. All you have to do is take a look at her Senate run.
32 Take a look at upstate New York.
33

1 **COOPER:** Your two minutes is up. Secretary Clinton, two
2 minutes?
3
4 **TRUMP:** It turned out to be a disaster.
5
6 **COOPER:** You have two minutes, Secretary Clinton.
7
8 **CLINTON:** Well, 67 percent of the people voted to re-elect
9 me when I ran for my second term, and I was very proud
10 and very humbled by that.
11
12 Mr. Carter, I have tried my entire life to do what I can to
13 support children and families. You know, right out of law
14 school, I went to work for the Children's Defense Fund.
15 And Donald talks a lot about, you know, the 30 years I've
16 been in public service. I'm proud of that. You know, I
17 started off as a young lawyer working against
18 discrimination against African-American children in schools
19 and in the criminal justice system. I worked to make sure
20 that kids with disabilities could get a public education,
21 something that I care very much about. I have worked with
22 Latinos — one of my first jobs in politics was down in
23 south Texas registering Latino citizens to be able to vote.
24 So I have a deep devotion, to use your absolutely correct
25 word, to making sure that an every American feels like he
26 or she has a place in our country.
27
28 And I think when you look at the letters that I get, a lot of
29 people are worried that maybe they wouldn't have a place
30 in Donald Trump's America. They write me, and one
31 woman wrote me about her son, Felix. She adopted him
32 from Ethiopia when he was a toddler. He's 10 years old
33 now. This is the only one country he's ever known. And he

1 listens to Donald on TV and he said to his mother one day,
2 will he send me back to Ethiopia if he gets elected?
3
4 You know, children listen to what is being said. To go back
5 to the very, very first question. And there's a lot of fear —
6 in fact, teachers and parents are calling it the Trump
7 effect. Bullying is up. A lot of people are feeling, you know,
8 uneasy. A lot of kids are expressing their concerns.
9
10 So, first and foremost, I will do everything I can to reach
11 out to everybody.
12
13 **COOPER:** Your time, Secretary Clinton.
14
15 **CLINTON:** Democrats, Republicans, independents, people
16 across our country. If you don't vote for me, I still want to
17 be your president.
18
19 **COOPER:** Your two minutes is up.
20
21 **CLINTON:** I want to be the best president I can be for
22 every American.
23
24 **COOPER:** Secretary Clinton, your two minutes is up. I want
25 to follow up on something that Donald Trump actually said
26 to you, a comment you made last month. You said that
27 half of Donald Trump's supporters are, quote,
28 "deplorables, racist, sexist, homophobic, xenophobic,
29 Islamophobic." You later said you regretted saying half.
30 You didn't express regret for using the term "deplorables."
31 To Mr. Carter's question, how can you unite a country if
32 you've written off tens of millions of Americans?
33

1 **CLINTON:** Well, within hours I said that I was sorry about
2 the way I talked about that, because my argument is not
3 with his supporters. It's with him and with the hateful and
4 divisive campaign that he has run, and the inciting of
5 violence at his rallies, and the very brutal kinds of
6 comments about not just women, but all Americans, all
7 kinds of Americans.
8
9 And what he has said about African-Americans and
10 Latinos, about Muslims, about POWs, about immigrants,
11 about people with disabilities, he's never apologized for.
12 And so I do think that a lot of the tone and tenor that he
13 has said — I'm proud of the campaign that Bernie Sanders
14 and I ran. We ran a campaign based on issues, not insults.
15 And he is supporting me 100 percent.
16
17 **COOPER:** Thank you.
18
19 **CLINTON:** Because we talked about what we wanted to
20 do. We might have had some differences, and we had a lot
21 of debates...
22
23 **COOPER:** Thank you, Secretary.
24
25 **TRUMP:** ... but we believed that we could make the
26 country better. And I was proud of that.
27
28 **COOPER:** I want to give you a minute to respond.
29
30 **TRUMP:** We have a divided nation. We have a very divided
31 nation. You look at Charlotte. You look at Baltimore. You
32 look at the violence that's taking place in the inner cities,
33 Chicago, you take a look at Washington, D.C.
34

1 We have an increase in murder within our cities, the
2 biggest in 45 years. We have a divided nation, because
3 people like her — and believe me, she has tremendous
4 hate in her heart. And when she said deplorables, she
5 meant it. And when she said irredeemable, they're
6 irredeemable, you didn't mention that, but when she said
7 they're irredeemable, to me that might have been even
8 worse.
9
10 **COOPER:** She said some of them are irredeemable.
11
12 **TRUMP:** She's got tremendous — she's got tremendous
13 hatred. And this country cannot take another four years of
14 Barack Obama, and that's what you're getting with her.
15
16 **COOPER:** Mr. Trump, let me follow up with you. In 2008,
17 you wrote in one of your books that the most important
18 characteristic of a good leader is discipline. You said, if a
19 leader doesn't have it, quote, "he or she won't be one for
20 very long." In the days after the first debate, you sent out
21 a series of tweets from 3 a.m. to 5 a.m., including one that
22 told people to check out a sex tape. Is that the discipline of
23 a good leader?
24
25 **TRUMP:** No, there wasn't check out a sex tape. It was just
26 take a look at the person that she built up to be this
27 wonderful Girl Scout who was no Girl Scout.
28
29 **COOPER:** You mentioned sex tape.
30
31 **TRUMP:** By the way, just so you understand, when she
32 said 3 o'clock in the morning, take a look at Benghazi. She
33 said who is going to answer the call at 3 o'clock in the

1 morning? Guess what? She didn't answer it, because when
2 Ambassador Stevens...
3
4 **COOPER:** The question is, is that the discipline of a good
5 leader?
6
7 **TRUMP:** ... 600 — wait a minute, Anderson, 600 times.
8 Well, she said she was awake at 3 o'clock in the morning,
9 and she also sent a tweet out at 3 o'clock in the morning,
10 but I won't even mention that. But she said she'll be
11 awake. Who's going — the famous thing, we're going to
12 answer our call at 3 o'clock in the morning. Guess what
13 happened? Ambassador Stevens — Ambassador Stevens
14 sent 600 requests for help. And the only one she talked to
15 was Sidney Blumenthal, who's her friend and not a good
16 guy, by the way. So, you know, she shouldn't be talking
17 about that.
18
19 Now, tweeting happens to be a modern day form of
20 communication. I mean, you can like it or not like it. I have,
21 between Facebook and Twitter, I have almost 25 million
22 people. It's a very effective way of communication. So you
23 can put it down, but it is a very effective form of
24 communication. I'm not un-proud of it, to be honest with
25 you.
26
27 **COOPER:** Secretary Clinton, does Mr. Trump have the
28 discipline to be a good leader?
29
30 **CLINTON:** No.
31
32 **TRUMP:** I'm shocked to hear that.
33
34   **(LAUGHTER)**

1
2 **CLINTON:** Well, it's not only my opinion. It's the opinion of
3 many others, national security experts, Republicans,
4 former Republican members of Congress. But it's in part
5 because those of us who have had the great privilege of
6 seeing this job up close and know how difficult it is, and
7 it's not just because I watched my husband take a $300
8 billion deficit and turn it into a $200 billion surplus, and 23
9 million new jobs were created, and incomes went up for
10 everybody. Everybody. African-American incomes went up
11 33 percent.
12
13 And it's not just because I worked with George W. Bush
14 after 9/11, and I was very proud that when I told him what
15 the city needed, what we needed to recover, he said
16 you've got it, and he never wavered. He stuck with me.
17
18 And I have worked and I admire President Obama. He
19 inherited the worst financial crisis since the Great
20 Depression. That was a terrible time for our country.
21
22 **COOPER:** We have to move along.
23
24 **CLINTON:** Nine million people lost their jobs.
25
26 **RADDATZ:** Secretary Clinton, we have to...
27
28 **CLINTON:** Five million homes were lost.
29
30 **RADDATZ:** Secretary Clinton, we're moving.
31
32 **CLINTON:** And $13 trillion in family wealth was wiped out.
33 We are back on the right track. He would send us back into

1 recession with his tax plans that benefit the wealthiest of
2 Americans.
3
4 **RADDATZ:** Secretary Clinton, we are moving to an
5 audience question. We're almost out of time. We have
6 another...
7
8 **TRUMP:** We have the slowest growth since 1929.
9
10 **RADDATZ:** We're moving to an audience question.
11
12 **TRUMP:** It is — our country has the slowest growth and
13 jobs are a disaster.
14
15 **RADDATZ:** Mr. Trump, Secretary Clinton, we want to get
16 to the audience. Thank you very much both of you.
17
18   **(LAUGHTER)**
19
20 We have another audience question. Beth Miller has a
21 question for both candidates.
22
23 **QUESTION:** Good evening. Perhaps the most important
24 aspect of this election is the Supreme Court justice. What
25 would you prioritize as the most important aspect of
26 selecting a Supreme Court justice?
27
28 **RADDATZ:** We begin with your two minutes, Secretary
29 Clinton.
30
31 **CLINTON:** Thank you. Well, you're right. This is one of the
32 most important issues in this election. I want to appoint
33 Supreme Court justices who understand the way the world
34 really works, who have real-life experience, who have not

1 just been in a big law firm and maybe clerked for a judge
2 and then gotten on the bench, but, you know, maybe they
3 tried some more cases, they actually understand what
4 people are up against.
5
6 Because I think the current court has gone in the wrong
7 direction. And so I would want to see the Supreme Court
8 reverse Citizens United and get dark, unaccountable
9 money out of our politics. Donald doesn't agree with that.
10
11 I would like the Supreme Court to understand that voting
12 rights are still a big problem in many parts of our country,
13 that we don't always do everything we can to make it
14 possible for people of color and older people and young
15 people to be able to exercise their franchise. I want a
16 Supreme Court that will stick with Roe v. Wade and a
17 woman's right to choose, and I want a Supreme Court that
18 will stick with marriage equality.
19
20 Now, Donald has put forth the names of some people that
21 he would consider. And among the ones that he has
22 suggested are people who would reverse Roe v. Wade and
23 reverse marriage equality. I think that would be a terrible
24 mistake and would take us backwards.
25
26 I want a Supreme Court that doesn't always side with
27 corporate interests. I want a Supreme Court that
28 understands because you're wealthy and you can give
29 more money to something doesn't mean you have any
30 more rights or should have any more rights than anybody
31 else.
32
33 So I have very clear views about what I want to see to kind
34 of change the balance on the Supreme Court. And I regret

1 deeply that the Senate has not done its job and they have
2 not permitted a vote on the person that President Obama,
3 a highly qualified person, they've not given him a vote to
4 be able to be have the full complement of nine Supreme
5 Court justices. I think that was a dereliction of duty.
6
7 I hope that they will see their way to doing it, but if I am so
8 fortunate enough as to be president, I will immediately
9 move to make sure that we fill that, we have nine justices
10 that get to work on behalf of our people.
11
12 **RADDATZ:** Thank you, Secretary Clinton. Thank you. You're
13 out of time. Mr. Trump?
14
15 **TRUMP:** Justice Scalia, great judge, died recently. And we
16 have a vacancy. I am looking to appoint judges very much
17 in the mold of Justice Scalia. I'm looking for judges — and
18 I've actually picked 20 of them so that people would see,
19 highly respected, highly thought of, and actually very
20 beautifully reviewed by just about everybody.
21
22 But people that will respect the Constitution of the United
23 States. And I think that this is so important. Also, the
24 Second Amendment, which is totally under siege by
25 people like Hillary Clinton. They'll respect the Second
26 Amendment and what it stands for, what it represents. So
27 important to me.
28
29 Now, Hillary mentioned something about contributions
30 just so you understand. So I will have in my race more than
31 $100 million put in — of my money, meaning I'm not
32 taking all of this big money from all of these different
33 corporations like she's doing. What I ask is this.
34

1 So I'm putting in more than — by the time it's finished, I'll
2 have more than $100 million invested. Pretty much self-
3 funding money. We're raising money for the Republican
4 Party, and we're doing tremendously on the small
5 donations, $61 average or so.
6
7 I ask Hillary, why doesn't — she made $250 million by
8 being in office. She used the power of her office to make a
9 lot of money. Why isn't she funding, not for $100 million,
10 but why don't you put $10 million or $20 million or $25
11 million or $30 million into your own campaign?
12
13 It's $30 million less for special interests that will tell you
14 exactly what to do and it would really, I think, be a nice
15 sign to the American public. Why aren't you putting some
16 money in? You have a lot of it. You've made a lot of it
17 because of the fact that you've been in office. Made a lot
18 of it while you were secretary of state, actually. So why
19 aren't you putting money into your own campaign? I'm
20 just curious.
21
22 **CLINTON:** Well...
23
24   **(CROSSTALK)**
25
26 **RADDATZ:** Thank you very much. We're going to get on to
27 one more question.
28
29 **CLINTON:** The question was about the Supreme Court. And
30 I just want to quickly say, I respect the Second
31 Amendment. But I believe there should be comprehensive
32 background checks, and we should close the gun show
33 loophole, and close the online loophole.
34

137

1   **COOPER:** Thank you.

2

3   **RADDATZ:** We have — we have one more question, Mrs.
4   Clinton.

5

6   **CLINTON:** We have to save as many lives as we possibly
7   can.

8

9   **COOPER:** We have one more question from Ken Bone
10 about energy policy. Ken?

11

12 QUESTION: What steps will your energy policy take to
13 meet our energy needs, while at the same time remaining
14 environmentally friendly and minimizing job loss for fossil
15 power plant workers?

16

17 **COOPER:** Mr. Trump, two minutes?

18

19 **TRUMP:** Absolutely. I think it's such a great question,
20 because energy is under siege by the Obama
21 administration. Under absolutely siege. The EPA,
22 Environmental Protection Agency, is killing these energy
23 companies. And foreign companies are now coming in
24 buying our — buying so many of our different plants and
25 then re-jiggering the plant so that they can take care of
26 their oil.

27

28 We are killing — absolutely killing our energy business in
29 this country. Now, I'm all for alternative forms of energy,
30 including wind, including solar, et cetera. But we need
31 much more than wind and solar.

32

33 And you look at our miners. Hillary Clinton wants to put all
34 the miners out of business. There is a thing called clean

1 coal. Coal will last for 1,000 years in this country. Now we
2 have natural gas and so many other things because of
3 technology. We have unbelievable — we have found over
4 the last seven years, we have found tremendous wealth
5 right under our feet. So good. Especially when you have
6 $20 trillion in debt.
7
8 I will bring our energy companies back. They'll be able to
9 compete. They'll make money. They'll pay off our national
10 debt. They'll pay off our tremendous budget deficits,
11 which are tremendous. But we are putting our energy
12 companies out of business. We have to bring back our
13 workers.
14
15 You take a look at what's happening to steel and the cost
16 of steel and China dumping vast amounts of steel all over
17 the United States, which essentially is killing our
18 steelworkers and our steel companies. We have to guard
19 our energy companies. We have to make it possible.
20
21 The EPA is so restrictive that they are putting our energy
22 companies out of business. And all you have to do is go to
23 a great place like West Virginia or places like Ohio, which is
24 phenomenal, or places like Pennsylvania and you see what
25 they're doing to the people, miners and others in the
26 energy business. It's a disgrace.
27
28 **COOPER:** Your time is up. Thank you.
29
30 **TRUMP:** It's an absolute disgrace.
31
32 **COOPER:** Secretary Clinton, two minutes.
33

1 **CLINTON:** And actually — well, that was very interesting.
2 First of all, China is illegally dumping steel in the United
3 States and Donald Trump is buying it to build his buildings,
4 putting steelworkers and American steel plants out of
5 business. That's something that I fought against as a
6 senator and that I would have a trade prosecutor to make
7 sure that we don't get taken advantage of by China on
8 steel or anything else.
9
10 You know, because it sounds like you're in the business or
11 you're aware of people in the business — you know that
12 we are now for the first time ever energy-independent.
13 We are not dependent upon the Middle East. But the
14 Middle East still controls a lot of the prices. So the price of
15 oil has been way down. And that has had a damaging
16 effect on a lot of the oil companies, right? We are,
17 however, producing a lot of natural gas, which serves as a
18 bridge to more renewable fuels. And I think that's an
19 important transition.
20
21 We've got to remain energy-independent. It gives us much
22 more power and freedom than to be worried about what
23 goes on in the Middle East. We have enough worries over
24 there without having to worry about that.
25
26 So I have a comprehensive energy policy, but it really does
27 include fighting climate change, because I think that is a
28 serious problem. And I support moving toward more clean,
29 renewable energy as quickly as we can, because I think we
30 can be the 21st century clean energy superpower and
31 create millions of new jobs and businesses.
32
33 But I also want to be sure that we don't leave people
34 behind. That's why I'm the only candidate from the very

1 beginning of this campaign who had a plan to help us
2 revitalize coal country, because those coal miners and
3 their fathers and their grandfathers, they dug that coal
4 out. A lot of them lost their lives. They were injured, but
5 they turned the lights on and they powered their factories.
6 I don't want to walk away from them. So we've got to do
7 something for them.
8
9 **COOPER:** Secretary Clinton...
10
11 **CLINTON:** But the price of coal is down worldwide. So we
12 have to look at this comprehensively.
13
14 **COOPER:** Your time is up.
15
16 **CLINTON:** And that's exactly what I have proposed. I hope
17 you will go to HillaryClinton.com and look at my entire
18 policy.
19
20 **COOPER:** Time is up. We have time for one more...
21
22 **RADDATZ:** We have...
23
24 **COOPER:** One more audience question.
25
26 **RADDATZ:** We've sneaked in one more question, and it
27 comes from Karl Becker.
28
29 **QUESTION:** Good evening. My question to both of you is,
30 regardless of the current rhetoric, would either of you
31 name one positive thing that you respect in one another?
32
33 **(APPLAUSE)**
34

1 **RADDATZ:** Mr. Trump, would you like to go first?

2

3 **CLINTON:** Well, I certainly will, because I think that's a very
4 fair and important question. Look, I respect his children.
5 His children are incredibly able and devoted, and I think
6 that says a lot about Donald. I don't agree with nearly
7 anything else he says or does, but I do respect that. And I
8 think that is something that as a mother and a
9 grandmother is very important to me.

10

11 So I believe that this election has become in part so — so
12 conflict-oriented, so intense because there's a lot at stake.
13 This is not an ordinary time, and this is not an ordinary
14 election. We are going to be choosing a president who will
15 set policy for not just four or eight years, but because of
16 some of the important decisions we have to make here at
17 home and around the world, from the Supreme Court to
18 energy and so much else, and so there is a lot at stake. It's
19 one of the most consequential elections that we've had.

20

21 And that's why I've tried to put forth specific policies and
22 plans, trying to get it off of the personal and put it on to
23 what it is I want to do as president. And that's why I hope
24 people will check on that for themselves so that they can
25 see that, yes, I've spent 30 years, actually maybe a little
26 more, working to help kids and families. And I want to take
27 all that experience to the White House and do that every
28 single day.

29

30 **RADDATZ:** Mr. Trump?

31

32 **TRUMP:** Well, I consider her statement about my children
33 to be a very nice compliment. I don't know if it was meant
34 to be a compliment, but it is a great — I'm very proud of

1 my children. And they've done a wonderful job, and
2 they've been wonderful, wonderful kids. So I consider that
3 a compliment.
4
5 I will say this about Hillary. She doesn't quit. She doesn't
6 give up. I respect that. I tell it like it is. She's a fighter. I
7 disagree with much of what she's fighting for. I do disagree
8 with her judgment in many cases. But she does fight hard,
9 and she doesn't quit, and she doesn't give up. And I
10 consider that to be a very good trait.
11
12 **RADDATZ:** Thanks to both of you.
13
14 **COOPER:** We want to thank both the candidates. We want
15 to thank the university here. This concludes the town hall
16 meeting. Our thanks to the candidates, the commission,
17 Washington University, and to everybody who watched.
18
19 **RADDATZ:** Please tune in on October 19th for the final
20 presidential debate that will take place at the University of
21 Nevada, Las Vegas. Good night, everyone.

THIRD

PRESIDENTIAL

DEBATE

1 **CHRIS WALLACE:** Good evening from the Thomas and
2 Mack Center at the University of Nevada, Las Vegas. I'm
3 Chris Wallace of Fox News and I welcome you to the third
4 and final of the 2016 presidential debates between
5 secretary of state Hillary Clinton and Donald J. Trump. This
6 debate is sponsored by the Commission on Presidential
7 Debates. The commission has designed the format. Six
8 roughly 15-minute segments, with two minute answers to
9 the first question then open discussion for the rest of each
10 segment. Both campaigns have agreed to those rules. For
11 the record, I decided the topics and the questions in each
12 topic. None of those questions has been shared with a
13 commission or the two candidates. The audience here in
14 the hall has promised to remain silent. No cheers, boos or
15 other interruptions so we and you can focus on what the
16 candidates have to say. No noise except right now as we
17 welcome the Democratic nominee for president, secretary
18 Clinton, and the Republican nominee for president, Mr.
19 Trump.
20
21 **WALLACE:** Secretary Clinton, Mr. Trump, welcome. Let's
22 get right to it. The first topic is the Supreme Court. You
23 both talked briefly about the court in the last debate, but I
24 want to drill down on this because the next president will
25 almost certainly have at least one appointment and likely

144

1 or possibly two or three appointments which means that
2 you will in effect determine the balance of the court for
3 what could be the next quarter century. First of all, where
4 do you want to see the court take the country? And
5 secondly, what's your view on how the constitution should
6 be interpreted? Do the founders' words mean what they
7 say or is it a living document to be applied flexibly,
8 according to changing circumstances? In this segment,
9 secretary Clinton, you go first. You have two minutes.
10
11 **CLINTON:** Thank you very much Chris and thanks to UNLV
12 for hosting us. You know, I think when we talk about the
13 Supreme Court, it really raises the central issue in this
14 election. Namely, what kind of country are we going to be?
15 What kind of opportunities will we provide for our
16 citizens? What kind of rights will Americans have? And I
17 feel strongly that the Supreme Court needs to stand on the
18 side of the American people. Not on the side of the
19 powerful corporations and the wealthy. For me, that
20 means that we need a Supreme Court that will stand up on
21 behalf of women's rights, on behalf of the rights of the
22 LGBT community, that will stand up and say no to Citizens
23 United, a decision that has undermined the election
24 system in our country because of the way it permits dark,
25 unaccountable money to come into our electoral system. I
26 have major disagreements with my opponent about these
27 issues and others that will be before the Supreme Court.
28 But I feel that at this point in our country's history, it is
29 important that we not reverse marriage equality, that we
30 not reverse Roe v. Wade, that we stand up against Citizens
31 United, we stand up for the rights of people in the
32 workplace, that we stand up and basically say, the
33 Supreme Court should represent all of us. That's how I see
34 the court. And the kind of people that I would be looking

1 to nominate to the court would be in the great tradition of
2 standing up to the powerful, standing up on behalf of our
3 rights as Americans. And I look forward to having that
4 opportunity. I would hope that the Senate would do its job
5 and confirm the nominee that President Obama has sent
6 to them. That's the way the constitution fundamentally
7 should operate. The President nominates and the Senate
8 advises and consents or not. But they go forward with the
9 process.
10
11 **WALLACE:** Secretary Clinton, thank you. Mr. Trump, same
12 question. Where do you want to see the court take the
13 country and how do you believe the constitution should be
14 interpreted?
15
16 **TRUMP:** Well, first of all, it's so great to be with you and
17 thank you, everybody. The Supreme Court, it is what it is
18 all about. Our country is so, so, it is just so imperative that
19 we have the right justices. Something happened recently
20 where Justice Ginsburg made some very inappropriate
21 statements toward me and toward a tremendous number
22 of people. Many, many millions of people that I represent
23 and she was forced to apologize. And apologize she did.
24 But these were statements that should never, ever have
25 been made. We need a Supreme Court that in my opinion
26 is going to uphold the second amendment and all
27 amendments, but the second amendment which is under
28 absolute siege. I believe, if my opponent should win this
29 race, which I truly don't think will happen, we will have a
30 second amendment which will be a very, very small replica
31 of what it is right now. But I feel that it is absolutely
32 important that we uphold because of the fact that it is
33 under such trauma. I feel that the justices that I am going
34 to appoint, and I've named 20 of them. The justices that I

1 am going to appoint will be pro-life. They will have a
2 conservative bent. They will be protecting the second
3 amendment. They are great scholars in all cases and
4 they're people of tremendous respect. They will interpret
5 the constitution the way the founders wanted it
6 interpreted and I believe that's very important. I don't
7 think we should have justices appointed that decide what
8 they want to hear. It is all about the constitution of, and it
9 is so important. The constitution the way it was meant to
10 be. And those are the people that I will appoint.
11
12 **WALLACE:** Mr. Trump, thank you. We now have about ten
13 minutes for an open discussion. I want to focus on two
14 issues that in fact, by the justices that you name, could
15 end up changing the existing law of the land. First, is one
16 that you mentioned Mr. Trump, and that is guns. Secretary
17 Clinton, you said last year, and let me quote: "The
18 Supreme Court is wrong on the second amendment." And
19 now, in fact, in the 2008 Heller case the court ruled that
20 there is a constitutional right to bear arms, but a right that
21 is reasonably limited. Those were the words of the judge
22 Antonin Scalia, who wrote the decision. What's wrong with
23 that?
24
25 **CLINTON:** Well, first of all, I support the second
26 amendment. I lived in Arkansas for 18 wonderful years. I
27 represented upstate New York. I understand and respect
28 the tradition of gun ownership that goes back to the
29 founding of our country, but I also believe that there can
30 be and must be reasonable regulation. Because I support
31 the second amendment doesn't mean that I want people
32 who shouldn't have guns to be able to threaten you, kill
33 you or members of your family. And so when I think about
34 what we need to do, we have 33,000 people a year who

147

1 die from guns. I think we need comprehensive background
2 checks, need to close the online loophole, close the gun
3 show loophole. There's other matters that I think are
4 sensible, that are the kinds of reforms that would make a
5 difference, that are not in any way conflicting with the
6 second amendment. You mentioned the Heller decision
7 and what I was saying that you referenced, Chris, was that
8 I disagreed with the way the court applied the second
9 amendment in that case. Because what the District of
10 Columbia was trying to do was to protect toddlers from
11 guns. And so they wanted people with guns to safely store
12 them. And the court did not accept that reasonable
13 regulation but they've accepted many others. So I see no
14 conflict between saving people's lives and defending the
15 second amendment.
16
17 **WALLACE:** Let me bring Mr. Trump in here. The bipartisan
18 debate coalition got millions of votes on questions to ask
19 here. And this was in fact one of the top questions that
20 they got. How will you ensure the second amendment is
21 protected? You just heard secretary Clinton's answer. Does
22 she persuade you that while you may disagree on
23 regulation, that in fact she in fact she supports the second
24 amendment right to bear arms.
25
26 **TRUMP:** Well the D.C. versus Heller decision was very
27 strongly... and she was extremely angry about it. I
28 watched. I mean, she was very, very angry when upheld.
29 And Justice Scalia was so involved and it was a well crafted
30 decision. But Hillary was extremely upset. Extremely angry.
31 And people that believe in the second amendment and
32 believe in it very strongly were very upset with what she
33 had to say.
34

148

1 **WALLACE:** Let me bring in secretary Clinton. Were you
2 extremely upset?
3
4 **CLINTON:** Well, I was upset because unfortunately, dozens
5 of toddlers injure themselves, even kill people with guns
6 because unfortunately, not everyone who has loaded guns
7 in their homes takes appropriate precautions. But there is
8 no doubt that I respect the second amendment. That I also
9 believe there is an individual right to bear arms. That is not
10 in conflict with sensible, common sense regulation. And
11 you know, look. I understand that Donald has been
12 strongly supported by the NRA, the gun lobby is on his
13 side. They're running millions of dollars of ads against me
14 and I regret that because what I would like to see is for
15 people to come together and say, of course we're going to
16 protect and defend the second amendment. But we're
17 going to do it in a way that tries to save some of these
18 33,000 lives that we lose every year.
19
20 **WALLACE:** Let me bring Mr. Trump back into this because
21 in fact, you oppose any limits on assault weapons, any
22 limits on high capacity magazines. You support a national
23 right-to-carry law. Why, sir?
24
25 **TRUMP:** Well, let me just tell you before we go any
26 further, in Chicago, which has the toughest gun laws in the
27 United States, probably you could say by far, they have
28 more gun violence than any other city. So we have the
29 toughest laws and you have tremendous gun violence. I
30 am a very strong supporter of the second amendment.
31 And I don't know if Hillary was saying it in a sarcastic
32 manner but I'm very proud to have the endorsement of
33 the NRA and it was the earliest endorsement they've ever
34 given to anybody who ran for president. So I'm very

1 honored by all of that. We are going to appoint justices,
2 this is the best way to help the second amendment. We
3 are going to appoint justices that will feel very strongly
4 about the second amendment. That will not do damage to
5 the second amendment.
6
7 **WALLACE:** Well, let's pick up on another issue which
8 divides you, and the justices that, whoever ends up
9 winning this election appoints, could have a dramatic
10 effect there. That's the issue of abortion. Mr. Trump,
11 you're pro-life. And I want to ask you specifically. Do you
12 want the court, including the justices that you will name,
13 to overturn Roe v. Wade, which includes, in fact, states a
14 woman's right to abortion.
15
16 **TRUMP:** Well, if that would happen, because I am pro-life
17 and I will be appointing pro-life judges, I would think that
18 would go back to the individual states.
19
20 **WALLACE:** I'm asking you specifically would you-
21
22 **TRUMP:** If they overturned it, it would go back to the
23 states.
24
25 **WALLACE:** But what I'm asking you, do you want to see the
26 court overturn it? You just said you want to see the court
27 protect the second amendment, do you want to see the
28 court overturn-
29
30 **TRUMP:** If we put another two or perhaps three justices
31 on, that is really what will happen. That will happen
32 automatically in my opinion. Because I am putting pro-life
33 justices on the court. I will say this. It will go back to the
34 states and the states will then make a determination.

1
2 **CLINTON:** Well, I strongly support Roe v. Wade which
3 guarantees a constitutional right to a woman to make the
4 most intimate, most difficult in many cases, decisions
5 about her health care that one can imagine. And in this
6 case, it is not only about Roe v. Wade. It is about what is
7 happening right now in America. So many states are
8 putting very stringent regulations on women that block
9 them from exercising that choice to the extent that they
10 are defunding planned parenthood which, of course
11 provides all kinds of cancer screenings and other benefits
12 for women in our country. Donald has said he is in favor of
13 defunding planned parenthood. He even supported
14 shutting the government down to defund planned
15 parenthood. I will defend planned parenthood. I will
16 defend Roe v. Wade and I will defend women's rights to
17 make their own healthcare decisions. We have come too
18 far to have that turn back now. And indeed, he said
19 women should be punished. There should be some form of
20 punishment for women who obtain abortions. And I could
21 just not be more opposed to that kind of thinking.
22
23 **WALLACE:** I'm going to give you a chance to respond. But I
24 wanted to ask you secretary Clinton, I want to explore how
25 far you think the right to abortion goes. You have been
26 quoted as saying that the fetus has no constitutional
27 rights. You also voted against a ban on late term partial
28 birth abortions. Why?
29
30 **CLINTON:** Because Roe v. Wade very clearly sets out that
31 there can be regulations on abortion so long as the life and
32 the health of the mother are taken into account. And
33 when I voted as a senator, I did not think that that was the
34 case. The kinds of cases that fall at the end of pregnancy

1 are often the most heartbreaking, painful decisions for
2 families to make. I have met with women who have,
3 toward the end of their pregnancy, get the worst news
4 one could get. That their health is in jeopardy if they
5 continue to carry to term. Or that something terrible has
6 happened or just been discovered about the pregnancy. I
7 do not think the United States government should be
8 stepping in and making those most personal of decisions.
9 So you can regulate if you are doing so with the life and
10 the health of the mother taken into account.
11
12 **WALLACE:** Mr. Trump, your reaction. Particularly on this
13 issue of late term partial birth abortions.
14
15 **TRUMP:** Well I think it is terrible. If you go with what
16 Hillary is saying, in the ninth month you can take baby and
17 rip the baby out of the womb of the mother just prior to
18 the birth of the baby. Now, you can say that that is okay
19 and Hillary can say that that is okay, but it's not okay with
20 me. Because based on what she is saying and based on
21 where she's going and where she's been, you can take
22 baby and rip the baby out of the womb. In the ninth
23 month. On the final day. And that's not acceptable.
24
25 **CLINTON:** Well that is not what happens in these cases.
26 And using that kind of scare rhetoric is just terribly
27 unfortunate. You should meet with some of the women
28 I've met with. Women I've known over the course of my
29 life. This is one of the worst possible choices that any
30 woman and her family has to make. And I do not believe
31 the government should be making it. You know, I've had
32 the great honor of traveling across the world on behalf of
33 our country. I've been to countries where governments
34 either forced women to have abortions, like they used to

1 do in China, or forced women to bear children like they
2 used to do in Romania. And I can tell you the government
3 has no business in the decisions that women make with
4 their families in accordance with their faith, with medical
5 advice. And I will stand up for that right.
6
7 **TRUMP:** And honestly, nobody has business doing what I
8 just said. Doing that as late as one or two or three or four
9 days prior to birth. Nobody has that.
10
11 **WALLACE:** All right. Let's move on to the subject of
12 immigration. And there is almost no issue that separates
13 the two of you more than the issue of immigration.
14 Actually there are many issues that separate the two of
15 you. Mr. Trump. You want to build a wall. Secretary
16 Clinton, you have offered no specific plan for how you
17 want to secure our southern border. Mr. Trump, you are
18 calling for major deportations. Secretary Clinton, you say
19 that within your first 100 days as president, you're going
20 to offer a package that includes a pathway to citizenship.
21 The question really is why are you right and your opponent
22 wrong? Mr. Trump, you go first in this segment, you have
23 two minutes.
24 **TRUMP:** Well first of all, she wants to give amnesty, which
25 is a disaster. And very unfair to all of the people waiting in
26 line for many, many years. We need strong borders. In the
27 audience we have four mothers of - I mean, these are
28 unbelievable people that I've gotten to know over a period
29 of years whose children have been killed, brutally killed, by
30 people that came into the country illegally. You have
31 thousands of mothers and fathers and relatives all over
32 the country.
33

1 They're coming in illegally. Drugs are pouring in through
2 the border. We have no country if we have no border.
3 Hillary wants to give amnesty. She wants to have open
4 borders. As you know, the border patrol agents, 16,500
5 plus I.C.E. last week endorsed me. First time they've
6 endorsed a candidate. It means their job is tougher. But
7 they know what's going on. They know it better than
8 anybody. They want strong borders. They feel we have to
9 have strong borders. I was up in New Hampshire the other
10 day. The biggest complaint they have, it's with all the
11 problems going on in the world, many of the problems
12 caused by Hillary Clinton and Barack Obama. All of the
13 problems. The single biggest problem is heroin that pours
14 across our southern borders. Just pouring and destroying
15 their youth It is poisoning the blood of their youth and
16 plenty of other people. We have to have strong borders.
17 We have to keep the drugs out of our country. Right now,
18 we're getting the drugs, they're getting the cash. We need
19 strong borders. We need absolute, we cannot give
20 amnesty. Now, I want to build the wall. We need the wall.
21 The border patrol, I.C.E., they all want the wall. We stop
22 the drugs; we shore up the border. One of my first acts will
23 be to get all of the drug lords, all of the bad ones, we have
24 some bad, bad people in this country that have to go out.
25 We're going to get them out. We're going to secure the
26 border. And once the border is secured, at a later date,
27 we'll make a determination as to the rest. But we have
28 some bad hombres here and we're going to get them out.
29
30 **WALLACE:** Mr. Trump, thank you. Same question to you,
31 secretary Clinton. Basically, why are you right and Mr.
32 Trump is wrong?
33

1 **CLINTON:** Well, as he was talking, I was thinking about a
2 young girl I met here in Las Vegas, Carla who is very
3 worried that her parents might be deported because she
4 was born in this country but they were not. They work
5 hard. They do everything they can to give her a good life.
6 And you're right. I don't want to rip families apart. I don't
7 want to be sending families away from children. I don't
8 want to see the deportation force that Donald has talked
9 about in action in our country. We have 11 million
10 undocumented people. They have 4 million American
11 citizen children. 15 million people. He said as recently as a
12 few weeks ago in Phoenix, that every undocumented
13 person would be subject to deportation. Here's with a that
14 means. It means you would have to have a massive law
15 enforcement presence where law enforcement officers
16 would be going school to school, home to home, business
17 to business. Rounding up people who are undocumented.
18 And we would then to have put them on trains, on buses
19 to get them out of our country. I think that is an idea that
20 is not in keeping with who we are as a nation. I think it is
21 an idea that would rip our country apart. I have been for
22 border security for years. I voted for border security in the
23 United States Senate. And my comprehensive immigration
24 reform plan, of course includes border security. But I want
25 to put our resources where I think they're most needed.
26 Getting rid of any violent person, anybody who should be
27 deported, we should deport them. When it comes to the
28 wall that Donald talks about building. He went to Mexico.
29 Had a meeting with the Mexican president. He didn't even
30 raise it. He choked. And then got into a Twitter war
31 because the Mexican president said we're not paying for
32 that wall. So I think we are both a nation of immigrants
33 and we are a nation of laws and that we can act
34 accordingly.   And   that's   why   I'm   introducing

1 comprehensive immigration reform within the first 100
2 days with a path to citizenship.
3
4 **WALLACE:** Thank you secretary Clinton. I want to follow-
5 up-
6
7 **TRUMP:** Chris, I think it's -- I think I should respond. First
8 of all, I had a very good meeting with the President of
9 Mexico. Very nice man. We will be doing very much better
10 with Mexico on trade deals. Believe me. The NAFTA deal
11 signed by her husband is one of the worst deals ever made
12 of any kind signed by anybody. It's a disaster. Hillary
13 Clinton wanted the wall. Hillary Clinton fought for the wall
14 in 2006 or there abouts. Now, she never gets anything
15 done, so naturally the wall wasn't built. But Hillary Clinton
16 wanted the wall.
17
18 **WALLACE:** Well, let me --
19
20 **TRUMP:** We are a country of laws. By the way --
21
22 **WALLACE:** I would like to hear from secretary Clinton.
23
24 **CLINTON:** I voted for border security and-
25
26 **TRUMP:** And a wall.
27
28 **CLINTON:** -There are some limited places where that was
29 appropriate. There also is necessarily going to be new
30 technology and how best to deploy that. But it is clear
31 when you look at what Donald has been proposing. He
32 started his campaign bashing immigrants, calling Mexican
33 immigrants rapists and criminals and drug dealers, that he
34 has a very different there view about what we should do

1 to deal with immigrants. Now, what I am also arguing is
2 that bringing undocumented immigrants out from the
3 shadows, putting them into the formal economy would be
4 good. Because then employers can't exploit them and
5 undercut Americans' wages. And Donald knows a lot about
6 this. He used undocumented labor to build the Trump
7 tower. He underpaid undocumented workers and when
8 they complained, he basically said what a lot of employers
9 do. You complain, I'll get you deported. I want to get
10 everybody out of the shadows. Get the economy working
11 and not let employers like Donald exploit undocumented
12 workers which hurts them but also hurts American
13 workers.
14
15 **TRUMP:** President Obama has moved millions of people
16 out. Nobody knows about it. Nobody talks about it. But
17 under Obama, millions of people have been moved out of
18 this country. They've been deported. She doesn't want to
19 say that, but that's what has happened and that's what
20 happened - big league. As far as moving these people out
21 and moving, we either have a country or we don't. We're a
22 country of laws. We either have a border or we don't.
23 Now, you can come back in and you can become a citizen.
24 But it's very unfair. We have millions of people that did it
25 the right way. They're on line. They're waiting. We're going
26 to speed up the process bigly, because it's very inefficient.
27 But they're on line and they're waiting to become citizens.
28 Very unfair that somebody runs across the border,
29 becomes a citizen. Under her plan you have open borders.
30 You would have a disaster on trade and … and you will
31 have a disaster with your open borders. What she doesn't
32 say is that President Obama has deported millions and
33 millions of people.
34

1 **WALLACE:** Secretary Clinton --

2

3 **CLINTON:** We will not have open borders. That is a rank
4 mischaracterization. We will have secure borders. But we
5 will also have reform. This used to be a bipartisan issue.
6 Ronald Reagan was the last president to sign --

7

8 **WALLACE:** Excuse me.

9

10 **CLINTON:** To sign immigration reform and George W. Bush
11 supported it as well.

12

13 **WALLACE:** Secretary Clinton, I want to clear up your
14 position on this issue because in a speech you gave to a
15 Brazilian bank for which you were paid $225,000, we've
16 learned from Wikileaks, that you said this. And I want to
17 quote. "My dream is a hemispheric common market with
18 open trade and open borders."

19

20 **TRUMP:** Thank you.

21

22 **WALLACE:** That's the question. Please, quiet, everybody. Is
23 that your dream? Open borders?

24

25 **CLINTON:** If you went on to read the rest of the sentence, I
26 was talking about energy. We trade more energy with our
27 neighbors than we trade with the rest of the world
28 combined. And I do want us to have an electric grid, an
29 energy system that crosses borders. I think that would be
30 a great benefit to us. But you are very clearly quoting from
31 WikiLeaks. What is really important about WikiLeaks is
32 that the Russian government has engaged in espionage
33 against Americans. They have hacked American websites,
34 American accounts of private people, of institutions. Then

1 they have given that information to WikiLeaks for the
2 purpose of putting it on the internet. This has come from
3 the highest levels of the Russian government. Clearly from
4 Putin himself in an effort, as 17 of our intelligence
5 agencies have confirmed, to influence our election. So I
6 actually think the most important question of this evening,
7 Chris, is finally, will Donald Trump admit and condemn
8 that the Russians are doing this, and make it clear that he
9 will not have the help of Putin in this election. That he
10 rejects Russian espionage against Americans, which he
11 actually encouraged in the past. Those are the questions
12 we need answered. We've never had anything like this
13 happen in any of our elections before.
14
15 **TRUMP:** That was a great pivot off the fact that she wants
16 open borders. Okay? How did we get on to Putin?
17
18 **WALLACE:** Hold on, folks. Because this is going to end up
19 getting out of control. Let's try to keep it quiet. For the
20 candidates and for the American people.
21
22 **TRUMP:** Just to finish on the borders, she wants open
23 borders. People are going to pour into our country. People
24 are going to come in from Syria. She wants 550% more
25 people than Barack Obama. And he has thousands and
26 thousands of people. They have no idea where they come
27 from. And you see, we are going to stop radical Islamic
28 terrorism in this country. She won't even mention the
29 words and neither will President Obama. So I just want to
30 tell you. She wants open borders. Now we can talk about
31 Putin. I don't know Putin. He said nice things about me. If
32 we got along well, that would be good. If Russia and the
33 United States got along well and went after ISIS, that
34 would be good. He has no respect for her. He has no

1 respect for our president. And I'll tell you what. We're in
2 very serious trouble. Because we have a country with
3 tremendous numbers of nuclear warheads, 1,800, by the
4 way. Where they expanded and we didn't. 1,800 nuclear
5 warheads. And she is playing chicken. Look.
6
7 **CLINTON:** Wait.
8
9 **TRUMP:** Putin from everything I see has no respect for this
10 person.
11
12 **CLINTON:** Well, that's because he would rather have a
13 puppet as president of the United States.
14
15 **TRUMP:** No puppet. You're the puppet.
16
17 **CLINTON:** It is pretty clear you won't admit that the
18 Russians have engaged in cyber-attacks against the United
19 States of America. That you encouraged espionage against
20 our people. That you are willing to spout the Putin line,
21 sign up for his wish list, break up NATO, do whatever he
22 wants to do. And that you continue to get help from him
23 because he has a very clear favorite in this race. So I think
24 that this is such an unprecedented situation. We've never
25 had a foreign government trying to interfere in our
26 election. We have 17, 17 intelligence agencies, civilian and
27 military who have all concluded that these espionage
28 attacks, these cyber-attacks, come from the highest levels
29 of the Kremlin. And they are designed to influence our
30 election. I find that deeply disturbing.
31
32 **WALLACE:** Secretary Clinton-
33
34 **CLINTON:** And I think it is time --

1

2 **TRUMP:** She has no idea whether it is Russia, China or
3 anybody else.

4

5 **CLINTON:** I am not quoting myself.

6

7 **TRUMP:** You have no idea.

8

9 **CLINTON:** I am quoting 17, 17 -- do you doubt?

10

11 **TRUMP:** Our country has no idea.

12

13 **CLINTON:** Our military and civilian -

14

15 **TRUMP:** Yeah, I doubt it, I doubt it.

16

17 **CLINTON:** He would rather believe Vladimir Putin than the
18 military and civilian intelligence professionals who are
19 sworn to protect us. I find that just absolutely --

20

21 **TRUMP:** She doesn't like Putin because Putin has
22 outsmarted her at every step of the way.

23

24 **WALLACE:** Mr. Trump-

25

26 **TRUMP:** Excuse me. Putin has outsmarted her in Syria,
27 he's outsmarted her every step of the way.

28

29 **WALLACE:** I do get to ask some questions. And I would like
30 to ask you this direct question. The top national security
31 officials of this country do believe that Russia has been
32 behind these hacks. Even if you don't know for sure
33 whether they are, do you condemn any interference by
34 Russia in the American election?

1

2 **TRUMP:** By Russia or anybody else.

3

4 **WALLACE:** Do you condemn their interference?

5

6 **TRUMP:** Of course I condemn, of course I condemn - I
7 don't know Putin. I have no idea-

8

9 **WALLACE:** I'm not asking you that.

10

11 **TRUMP:** I never met Putin. This is not my best friend. But if
12 the United States got along with Russia, it wouldn't be so
13 bad. Let me tell you, Putin has outsmarted her and Obama
14 at every single step of the way. Whether it is Syria. You
15 name it. Missiles. Take a look at the start-up that they
16 signed. The Russians have said, according to many, many
17 reports, I can't believe they allowed us to do this. They
18 create warheads and we can't. The Russians can't believe
19 it. She has been outsmarted by Putin and all you have to
20 do is look at the Middle East. They've taken over. We've
21 spent $6 trillion. They've taken over the Middle East. She
22 has been outsmarted and outplayed worse than anybody
23 I've ever seen in any government whatsoever.

24

25 **WALLACE:** We're a long way away from immigration. I'm
26 going to let you finish this. You have about 45 seconds.

27

28 **TRUMP:** And she always will be.

29

30 **CLINTON:** I find it ironic that he is raising nuclear weapons.
31 This is a person who has been very cavalier, even casual
32 about the use of nuclear weapons.

33

34 **TRUMP:** Wrong.

1
2 **CLINTON:** He has advocated more countries getting them.
3 Japan, Korea, even Saudi Arabia. He's said if we have
4 them, why don't we use them which I think is terrifying.
5 But here's the deal. The bottom line on nuclear weapons is
6 that when the president gives the order, it must be
7 followed. There is about four minutes between the order
8 being given and the people responsible for launching
9 nuclear weapons to do so. And that is why ten people who
10 have had that awesome responsibility have come out and
11 in an unprecedented way said they would not trust Donald
12 Trump with the nuclear codes or to have his finger on the
13 nuclear button.
14
15 **TRUMP:** I have 200 generals and admirals, 21 endorsing
16 me. 21 congressional medal of honor recipients. As far as
17 Japan and other countries, we are being ripped off by
18 everybody in the world. We're defending other countries.
19 We are spending a fortune doing it. They have the bargain
20 of the century. All I said is we have to renegotiate these
21 agreements. Because our country cannot afford to defend
22 Saudi Arabia, Japan, Germany, South Korea, and many
23 other places. We cannot continue to afford. She took that
24 as saying nuclear weapons.
25
26 **WALLACE:** Okay.
27
28 **TRUMP:** Look. She's been proven to be a liar on so many
29 different ways. This is just another lie.
30
31 **CLINTON:** Well, I'm just quoting you when-
32
33 **TRUMP:** There is no quote. You won't find a quote from
34 me.

1

2 **CLINTON:** Nuclear competition in Asia. You said go ahead.
3 Enjoy yourselves, folks.

4

5 **TRUMP:** And defend yourselves. And defend yourselves. I
6 didn't say -- and defend yourself.

7

8 **CLINTON:** The United States has kept the peace through
9 our alliances. Donald wants to tear up our alliances. I think
10 it makes the world safer and frankly, it makes the United
11 States safer. I would work with our allies in Asia, in Europe,
12 in the Middle East and elsewhere. That is the only way --

13

14 **WALLACE:** We are going to move on to the next topic
15 which is the economy. And I hope we handle that as well
16 as we did immigration. You also have very different ideas
17 about how to get the economy growing faster. Secretary
18 Clinton, in your plan, government plays a big role. You see
19 more government spending, more entitlements, more tax
20 credits, more tax penalties. Mr. Trump, you want to get
21 government out with lower taxes and less regulation.
22 We're going to drill down into this a little bit more. In this
23 overview, please explain to me why you believe your plan
24 will create more jobs and growth for this country and your
25 opponent's plan will not. In this round, you go first,
26 secretary Clinton.

27

28 **CLINTON:** Well I think the middle class thrives, America
29 thrives. So my plan is based on growing the economy,
30 giving middle class families many more opportunities. I
31 want us to have the biggest jobs program since World War
32 II. Jobs in infrastructure and advanced manufacturing. I
33 think we can compete with high wage countries and I
34 believe we should. New jobs in clean energy. Not only to

1 fight climate change, which is a serious problem but to
2 create new opportunities and new businesses. I want us to
3 do more to help small business, that's where two-thirds of
4 the new jobs are going to come from. I want to us raise the
5 national minimum wage because people who work full
6 time should not still be in poverty. And I sure do want to
7 make sure women get equal pay for the work we do. I feel
8 strongly that we have to have an education system that
9 starts with preschool and goes through college. That's why
10 I want more technical education and community colleges,
11 real apprenticeships to prepare young peel for the jobs of
12 the future. I want to make college debt-free and for
13 families making less than $125,000, you will not get a
14 tuition bill from a public college or a university if the plan
15 that I worked on with Bernie Sanders is enacted. And
16 we're going to work hard to make sure that it is. Because
17 we are going to go where the money is. Most of the gains
18 in the last years since the great recession have gone to the
19 very top. So we are going to have the wealthy pay their
20 fair share. We're going to have corporations make a
21 contribution greater than they are now to our country.
22 That is a plan that has been analyzed by independent
23 experts which said that it could produce 10 million new
24 jobs. By contrast, Donald's plan has been analyzed to
25 conclude it might lose 3.5 million jobs. Why? Because his
26 whole plan is to cut taxes. To give the biggest tax breaks
27 ever to the wealthy and to corporations. Adding $20
28 trillion to our debt and causing the kind of dislocation that
29 we have seen before. Because it truly will be trickle down
30 economics on steroids. So the plan I have I think will
31 actually produce greater opportunities. The plan he has
32 will cost us jobs and possibly lead to another great
33 recession.
34

1 **WALLACE:** Secretary, thank you Mr. Trump, why will your
2 plan create more jobs and growth than secretary Clinton?
3
4 **TRUMP:** Well, first of all, before I start on my plan, her
5 plan is going to raise taxes and even double your taxes.
6 Her tax plan is a disaster. And she can say all she wants
7 about college tuition. And I'm a big proponent. We're
8 going to do a lot of things for college tuition but the rest
9 the public is going to be paying for it. We will have a
10 massive, massive tax increase under Hillary Clinton's plan.
11 But I would like to start off where we left. Because when I
12 said Japan and Germany and I'm not just singling them
13 out. But South Korea, these are very rich countries. Saudi
14 Arabia. Nothing but money. We protect Saudi Arabia. Why
15 aren't they paying? She immediately, when she heard this,
16 I questioned it, and I questioned NATO, why aren't they
17 NATO questioned? Why aren't they paying? Because they
18 weren't paying. Since I did this, this was a year ago. All of a
19 sudden they're paying. And I've been given a lot of credit
20 for it. All of a sudden, they're starting to pay up. They have
21 to pay up. We're protecting people. They have to pay up.
22 And I'm a big fan of NATO but they have to pay up. She
23 comes out and says "we love our allies. We think our allies
24 are great." Well, it is awfully hard to get them to pay up
25 when you have somebody saying we think how great they
26 are. We have to tell Japan in a very nice way, we have to
27 tell Germany, all of these countries, South Korea. We have
28 to say, you have to help us out. We have, during his
29 regime, during President Obama's regime, we've doubled
30 our national debt. We're up to $20 trillion. So my plan,
31 we're going to negotiate trade deals. We're going to have
32 a lot of free trade. More free trade than we have right
33 now. But we have horrible deals. Our jobs are being taken
34 out by the deal that her husband signed. NAFTA. One of

1 the worst deals ever. The jobs are being sucked out of our
2 economy. You look at the places I just left. You go to
3 Pennsylvania, you go to Ohio, you go to Florida, you go to
4 any of them. You go to upstate New York. Our jobs have
5 fled to Mexico and other places. We're bringing our jobs
6 back. I'm going to renegotiate NAFTA. And if I can't make a
7 great deal, then we're going to terminate NAFTA and
8 we're going to create new deals. We're going to have
9 trade but we're going to terminate it. We're going on
10 make a great trade deal. If we can't, we're going to go our
11 separate way because it has been a disaster. We're going
12 to cut taxes massively. We're going to cut business taxes
13 massively. They're going to start hiring people we're going
14 to bring the $2.5 trillion that's offshore back into the
15 country. We are going to start the engine rolling again
16 because right now, our country is dying. At 1% GDP.
17
18 **CLINTON:** Let me translate that if I can, Chris.
19
20 **TRUMP:** You can't.
21
22 **CLINTON:** The fact is, he is going to advocate for the
23 largest tax cuts we've ever seen. Three times more than
24 the tax cuts under the Bush administration. I have said
25 repeatedly throughout this campaign; I will not raise taxes
26 on anyone making $250,000 or less. I also will not add a
27 penny to the debt. I have costed out what I'm going to do.
28 He will, through his massive tax cuts, add $20 trillion to the
29 debt. He mentioned the debt. We know how to get control
30 of the debt. When my husband was president, we went
31 from a $300 billion deficit to a $200 billion surplus and we
32 were actually on the path to eliminating the national debt.
33 When President Obama came into office, he inherited the
34 worst economic disaster since the great depression. He

1 has cut the deficit by two-thirds. So yes, one of the ways
2 you go after the debt, one of the ways you create jobs is
3 by investing in people. So I do have investments.
4 Investments in new jobs, investments in education, skill
5 training, and the opportunities for people to get ahead
6 and stay ahead. That's the kind of approach--
7
8 **WALLACE:** Secretary --
9
10 **CLINTON:** -- that will work. Cutting taxes on the wealthy.
11 We've tried that. It has not worked the way that it has
12 been --
13
14 **WALLACE:** Secretary Clinton, I want to pursue your plan
15 because in many ways, it is similar to the Obama stimulus
16 plan in 2009, which has led to the slowest GDP growth
17 since 1949.
18
19 **TRUMP:** Correct.
20
21 **WALLACE:** Thank you, sir. You told me in July when we
22 spoke that the problem is that President Obama didn't get
23 to do enough in what he was trying to do with the
24 stimulus. So is your plan basically more, even more of the
25 Obama stimulus?
26
27 **CLINTON:** Well, it is a combination, Chris. Let me say that
28 when you inherit the level of economic catastrophe that
29 President Obama inherited, it was a real touch and go
30 situation. I was in the Senate before I became secretary of
31 state. I've never seen people as physically distraught as the
32 Bush administration team was because of what was
33 happening to the economy. I personally believe that the
34 steps that President Obama took saved the economy. He

1 doesn't get the credit he deserves for taking some very
2 hard positions.
3
4 But it was a terrible recession. So now we've dug ourselves
5 out of it. We're standing, but we're not yet running. So
6 what I am proposing is that we invest from the middle out,
7 and the ground up. Not the top down. That is not going to
8 work. That is why what I have put forward doesn't add a
9 penny to the debt. But it is the kind of approach that will
10 enable more people to take those new jobs, higher paying
11 jobs. We're beginning to see some increase in incomes.
12 And we certainly have had a long string of increasing jobs.
13 We have got to do more to get the whole economy
14 moving and that's what I believe I will be able to do.
15
16 **WALLACE:** Mr. Trump, even conservative economists who
17 have looked at your plan say that the numbers don't add
18 up. That your idea, and you've talked about 25 million jobs
19 created. 4% growth-
20
21 **TRUMP:** Over a 10-year period.
22
23 **WALLACE:** -- is unrealistic. And they say, you talk a lot
24 about growing the energy industry. They say with oil prices
25 as low as they are right now, that's unrealistic as well. Your
26 response?
27
28 **TRUMP:** So I just left some high representatives of India.
29 They're growing at 8%. China is growing at 7%. And that
30 for them is a catastrophically low number. We are growing
31 our last report came out, and it is right around the 1%
32 level. And I think it's going down. Last week as you know,
33 the end of last week, they came out with an anemic jobs
34 report. A terrible jobs report. In fact, I said is that the last

1 jobs report before the election? Because if it is, I should
2 win easily because it was so bad. The report was so bad.
3 Look, our country is stagnant. We've lost our jobs, we've
4 lost our businesses. We're not making things anymore,
5 relatively speaking. Our product is pouring in from China,
6 pouring in from Vietnam, pouring in from all over the
7 world. I've visited so many communities. This has been
8 such an incredible education for me, Chris. I've gotten to
9 know so many, I've developed so many friends over the
10 last year. And they cry when they see what has happened.
11 I pass factories that were thriving, 20, 25 years ago and
12 because of the bill her husband signed and that she
13 blessed 100%. It is just horrible what has happened to
14 these people in these communities. Now, she can say her
15 husband did well but boy, did they suffer as NAFTA kicked
16 in because it didn't really kick in very much. But it kicked in
17 after they left. Boy, did they suffer. That was one of the
18 worst things that has ever been signed by our country.
19 Now she wants to sign Trans-Pacific Partnership. And she
20 wants it. She lied when she said she didn't call it the gold
21 standard in one of the debates. She totally lied. She did
22 call it the gold standard. And they actually fact checked
23 and they said I was right.
24
25 **WALLACE:** I want to give you a chance to briefly speak to
26 that then I want to pivot -- to Obamacare. But go ahead.
27 Briefly.
28
29 **TRUMP:** And that will be as bad as NAFTA.
30
31 **CLINTON:** Well, first, let me say, number one, when I saw
32 the final agreement for TPP, I said I was against it. It didn't
33 meet my test. I've had the same test. Does it create jobs,
34 raise incomes and further our national security. I'm against

1 it now. I'll be against it after the election. I'll be against it
2 when I'm president. There's only one of us on this stage
3 who has actually shipped jobs to Mexico because that's
4 Donald. He has shipped jobs to 12 countries including
5 Mexico. But he mentioned China. And, you know, one of
6 the biggest problems we have with China is the illegal
7 dumping of steel and aluminum into our markets. I have
8 fought against that as a senator. I have stood up against it
9 as Secretary of State. Donald has bought Chinese steel and
10 aluminum. In fact, the Trump Hotel right here in Las Vegas
11 was made with Chinese steel. So he goes around with
12 crocodile tears about how terrible it is. But he has given
13 jobs to Chinese steelworkers, not American steelworkers.
14 That's the kind of approach that is just not going to work.
15 We're going to pull the country together. We're going to
16 have trade agreements that we enforce. That's why I'm
17 going to have a trade prosecutor for the first time in
18 history. And we're going to enforce those agreements and
19 we're going to look for businesses to help us by buying
20 American products.
21
22 **TRUMP:** Can I ask a simple question? She's been doing this
23 for 30 years. Why the hell didn't you do it over the last 15,
24 20 years? You were very much involved.
25
26 **CLINTON:** I voted --
27
28 **TRUMP:** Excuse me. My turn. You were very much
29 involved in every aspect of this country. Very much. And
30 you do have experience. I say the one thing you have over
31 me is experience. But it is bad experience because what
32 you've done has turned out badly. For 30 years you've
33 been in a position to help. And if you say that I used steel
34 or I used something else, I- make it impossible for me to

1 do. I wouldn't mind. The problem is, you talk but you don't
2 get anything done, Hillary. You don't. Just like when you
3 ran the State Department, $6 billion was missing. How do
4 you miss $6 billion? You ran the State department. $6
5 billion was either stolen, they don't know. It's gone. $6
6 billion. If you become president, this country is going to be
7 in some mess. Believe me.
8
9 **CLINTON:** Well, first of all, what he just said about the
10 State Department is not only untrue, it's been debunked
11 numerous times. but I think it's really an important issue.
12 He raised the 30 years of experience, so let me just talk
13 briefly about that. You know, back in the 1970s, I worked
14 for the children's defense fund and I was taking on
15 discrimination against African-American kids in schools. He
16 was getting sued by the Justice Department for racial
17 discrimination in his apartment buildings. In the 1980s, I
18 was working to reform the schools in Arkansas. He was
19 borrowing $14 million from his father to start his
20 businesses. In the 1990s, I went to Beijing and I said
21 women's rights are human rights. He insulted a former
22 Miss Universe, Alicia Machado, and called her an eating
23 machine.
24
25 **TRUMP:** Give me a break.
26
27 **CLINTON:** And on the day when I was in the situation room
28 monitoring the raid that brought Osama bin laden to
29 justice, he was hosting The Celebrity Apprentice. So I'm
30 happy to compare my 30 years of experience, what I've
31 done for this country, trying to help in every way I could,
32 especially kids and families, get ahead and stay ahead,
33 with your thirty years and I'll let the American people
34 make that decision.

1
2 **TRUMP:** Well I think I did a much better job. I built a
3 massive company, a great company, some of the greatest
4 assets anywhere in the world worth many, many billions of
5 dollars. I started with a $1 million loan. I agree with that.
6 It's a $1 million loan, but I built a phenomenal company.
7 And if we could run our country the way I've run my
8 company, we would have a country that would you would
9 be so proud of, you would even be proud of it. And frankly,
10 when you look at her real record, take a look at Syria, take
11 a look at the migration, take a look at Libya, take a look at
12 Iraq. She gave us ISIS because her and Obama created this
13 huge vacuum, and a small group came out of that huge
14 vacuum because, we should have never been in Iraq, but
15 once we were there, we should have never got out the
16 way they wanted to get out. She gave us ISIS as sure as
17 you are sitting there. And what happened is now ISIS is in
18 32 countries. Now I listen to how she's going to get rid of
19 ISIS. She's going to get to rid of nobody.
20
21 **WALLACE:** We're going to get to foreign hot spots in a few
22 moments, but the next segment is fitness to be president
23 of the United States. Mr. Trump, at the last debate, you
24 said your talk about grabbing women was just that, talk,
25 and that you'd never actually done it. And since then, as
26 we all know, nine women have come forward and said
27 that you either groped them or kissed them without their
28 consent. Why would so many different women from so
29 many different circumstances over so many different
30 years, why would they all in this last couple of weeks make
31 up -- you deny this. Why would they make up these
32 stories? And since this is a question for both of you,
33 secretary Clinton, Mr. Trump says what your husband did

1 and what you defended was even worse. Mr. Trump, you
2 go first.
3
4 **TRUMP:** Well, first of all, those stories have been largely
5 debunked. Those people, I don't know those people. I have
6 a feeling how they came. I believe it was her campaign
7 that did it just like if you look at what came out today on
8 the clips where I was wondering what happened with my
9 rally in Chicago and other rallies where we had such
10 violence. She's the one and Obama that caused the
11 violence. They hired people. They paid them $1500, and
12 they're on tape saying be violent, cause fights, do bad
13 things. I would say the only way -- because those stories
14 are all totally false. I have to say that, and I didn't even
15 apologize to my wife who is sitting right here because I
16 didn't do anything. I didn't know any of these women. I
17 didn't see these women. These women, the woman on the
18 plane, the woman on the - I think they want either fame or
19 her campaign did it. And I think it's her campaign because
20 what I saw what they did, which is a criminal act, by the
21 way, where they're telling people to go out and start
22 fistfights and start violence -- and I'll tell you what. In
23 particular, in Chicago, people were hurt and people could
24 have killed in that riot. And that's now all on tape started
25 by her. I believe, Chris, she got these people to step
26 forward. If it wasn't, they get their ten minutes of fame,
27 but they were all totally -- it was all fiction. It was lies and
28 it was fiction.
29
30 **CLINTON:** Well --
31
32 **WALLACE:** Secretary Clinton?
33

174

1 **CLINTON:** At the last debate, we heard Donald talking
2 about what he did to women, and after that a number of
3 women have come forward saying that's exactly what he
4 did to them. Now, what was his response? Well, he held a
5 number of big rallies where he said that he could not
6 possibly have done those things to those women because
7 they were not attractive enough for –
8
9 **TRUMP:** I did not say that.
10
11 **CLINTON:** -- them to be assaulted.
12
13 **TRUMP:** I did not say that.
14
15 **CLINTON:** In fact, he went on to say --
16
17 **WALLACE:** Her two minutes. Sire, her two minutes.
18
19 **TRUMP:** I did not say that.
20
21 **WALLACE:** Her two minutes.
22
23 **CLINTON:** He went on to say "look at her, I don't think so."
24 About another woman, he said "that wouldn't be my first
25 choice." He attacked the woman reporter writing the
26 story, called her disgusting, as he has called a number of
27 women during this campaign. Donald thinks belittling
28 women makes him bigger. He goes after their dignity, their
29 self-worth, and I don't think there is a woman anywhere
30 that doesn't know what that feels like. So we now know
31 what Donald thinks and what he says and how he acts
32 toward women. That's who Donald is. I think it's really up
33. to all of us to demonstrate who we are and who our
34 country is and to stand up and be very clear about what

1 we expect from our next president, how we want to bring
2 our country together, where we don't want to have the
3 kind of pitting of people one against the other, where
4 instead we celebrate our diversity, we lift people up, and
5 we make our country even greater. America is great
6 because America is good. And it really is up to all of us to
7 make that true now and in the future and particularly for
8 our children and our grandchildren.
9
10 **WALLACE:** Mr. Trump --
11
12 **TRUMP:** Nobody has more respect for women than I do.
13 Nobody.
14
15 **(LAUGHTER)**
16
17 **WALLACE:** Please, everybody.
18
19 **TRUMP:** And frankly, those stories have been largely
20 debunked. And I really want to just talk about something
21 slightly different. She mentions this, which is all fiction, all
22 fictionalized, probably or possibly started by her and her
23 very sleazy campaign. But I will tell you what isn't
24 fictionalized are her e-mails where she destroyed 33,000
25 e-mails criminally, criminally after getting a subpoena from
26 the United States Congress. What happened to the FBI, I
27 don't know. We have a great general, four-star general,
28 today you read it in all the papers going to potentially
29 serve five years in jail for lying to the FBI, one lie. She's lied
30 hundreds of times to the people, to Congress, and to the
31 FBI. He's going to probably go to jail. This is a four-star
32 general, and she gets away with it and she can run for the
33 presidency of the United States? That's really what you
34 should be talking about, not fiction where somebody

1 wants fame or where they come out of her crooked
2 campaign.
3
4 **WALLACE:** Secretary Clinton?
5
6 **CLINTON:** Well, every time Donald is pushed on
7 something, which is obviously uncomfortable like what
8 these women are saying, he immediately goes to denying
9 responsibility and it's not just about women. He never
10 apologizes or says he's sorry for anything, so we know
11 what he has said and what he's done to women. But he
12 also went after a disabled reporter, mocked and mimicked
13 him on national television.
14
15 **TRUMP:** Wrong.
16
17 **CLINTON:** He went after Mr. And Mrs. Khan, the parents of
18 a young man who died serving our country, a gold star
19 family because of their religion. He went after John
20 McCain, a prisoner of war, said he prefers people that
21 aren't captured. He went after a federal judge born in
22 Indiana but who Donald said couldn't be trusted to try the
23 fraud and racketeering case against Trump University
24 because his parents were Mexican. So it's not one thing.
25 This is a pattern, a pattern of divisiveness, of a very dark
26 and in many ways dangerous vision of our country where
27 he incites violence, where he applauds people who are
28 pushing and pulling and punching at his rallies. That is not
29 who America is, and I hope that as we move in the last
30 weeks of this campaign more and more people will
31 understand what's at stake in this election. It really does
32 come down to what kind of country we are going to have.
33

1 **TRUMP:** So sad when she talks about violence at my rallies
2 and she caused the violence. It's on tape. The other things
3 are false, but honestly I'd love to talk about getting rid of
4 ISIS and I'd love to talk about other things.
5
6 **WALLACE:** Okay.
7
8 **TRUMP:** But those other charges, as she knows, are false.
9
10 **WALLACE:** In this bucket about fitness to be president
11 there's been a lot of developments over the last ten days
12 since the last debate. I'd like to ask you about them. These
13 are questions that the American people have. Secretary
14 Clinton, during your 2009 Senate confirmation hearing you
15 promised to avoid even the appearance of a conflict of
16 interest with your dealing with the Clinton Foundation
17 while you were secretary of state, but e-mails show that
18 donors got speciall access to you, those seeking grants for
19 Haiti relief separately from non-donors and some of those
20 donors got contracts, government contracts, taxpayer
21 money. Can you really say you've kept your pledge to that
22 Senate committee and why isn't what happened and what
23 went on and between you and the Clinton Foundation?
24 Why isn't it what Mr. Trump calls pay-to-play?
25
26 **CLINTON:** Well, everything I did as secretary of state was
27 in furtherance of our country's interests and our values.
28 The state department has said that. I think that's been
29 proven, but I am happy -- in fact, I'm thrilled to talk about
30 the Clinton Foundation because it is a world renowned
31 charity and I'm so proud of the work that it does. I could
32 talk for the rest of the debate. I know I don't have the time
33 to do that, but just briefly the Clinton Foundation made it
34 possible for 11 million people around the world with HIV

1 AIDS to afford treatment and that's about half of all the
2 people in the world that are getting treatment in
3 partnership with the American health association.
4
5 **WALLACE:** Secretary Clinton, respectfully, this is an open
6 discussion.
7
8 **CLINTON:** Well, it is an open discussion.
9
10 **WALLACE:** The specific question is about pay to play --
11
12 **CLINTON:** There is a lot of evidence about the very good
13 work --
14
15 **TRUMP:** And it's a criminal enterprise --
16
17 **WALLACE:** Please let Mr. Trump speak.
18
19 **TRUMP:** It's a criminal enterprise. Saudi Arabia given $25
20 million, Qatar, all of these countries. You talk about
21 women and women's rights? So these are people that
22 push gays off business, off buildings. These are people that
23 kill women and treat women horribly and yet you take
24 their money. So I'd like to ask you right now why don't you
25 give back the money that you've taken from certain
26 countries that treat certain groups of people so horribly?
27 Why don't you give back the money? I think it would be a
28 great gesture because she takes a tremendous amount of
29 money. And you take a look at the people of Haiti. I was in
30 Little Haiti the other day in Florida, and I want to tell you
31 they hate the Clintons because what's happened in Haiti
32 with the Clinton Foundation is a disgrace. And you know it
33 and they know it and everybody knows it.
34

1   **WALLACE:** Secretary Clinton?

2

3   **CLINTON:** Well, very quickly, we at the Clinton Foundation
4   spend 90%, 90%, of all the money that is donated on
5   behalf of programs for people around the world and in our
6   own country. I'm very proud of that. We have the highest
7   rating from the watchdogs that follow foundations. And I
8   would be happy to compare what we do with the Trump
9   Foundation which took money from other people and
10 bought a six-foot portrait of Donald. I mean, who does
11 that? I mean, it just was astonishing. But when it comes to
12 Haiti, Haiti is the poorest country in our hemisphere. The
13 earthquake and the hurricanes, it has devastated Haiti. Bill
14 and I have been involved in trying to help Haiti for many
15 years. The Clinton Foundation raised $30 million to help
16 Haiti after the catastrophic earthquake and all of the
17 terrible problems the people there had. We've done things
18 to help small businesses, agriculture, and so much else.
19 And we're going to keep working to help Haiti because it is
20 an important part of the American experience.

21

22 **TRUMP:** I don't want you to help them anymore. I'd like to
23 mention one thing. Trump Foundation, small foundation.
24 People contribute. I contribute. The money goes, 100%,
25 100% goes to different charities, including a lot of military.
26 I don't get anything. I don't buy boats. I don't buy planes.

27

28 **WALLACE:** Wasn't some of the money used to settle your
29 lawsuit, sir?

30

31 **TRUMP:** No, we put up the American flag and that's it.
32 They put up the American flag. We fought for the right in
33 Palm Beach to put up the American flag.

34

1 **WALLACE:** There was a penalty that was imposed by Palm
2 Beach county --
3
4 **TRUMP:** There was, there was and by the way, the money
5 went to fisher house where they build houses, the money
6 that you're talking about went to fisher house where they
7 build houses for veterans and disabled veterans.
8
9 **CLINTON:** Of course, there's no way we can know whether
10 any of that is true because he hasn't released his tax
11 returns. He's the first candidate ever to run for president
12 in the last 40-plus years who has not released his tax
13 returns. So everything he says about charity or anything
14 else, we can't prove it. You can look at our tax returns.
15 We've got them all out there. What is really troubling is
16 that we learned in the last debate he has not paid a penny
17 in federal income tax. And we were talking about
18 immigrants a few minutes ago, Chris. Half of all
19 undocumented immigrants actually pay federal income
20 tax. So we have undocumented immigrants in America
21 who are paying more federal income tax than a billionaire.
22 I find that just astonishing.
23
24 **TRUMP:** We're entitled because of the laws that people
25 like her pass to take massive amounts of depreciation on
26 other charges and we do it. And all of her donors, just
27 about all of them. I know Buffett took hundreds of millions
28 of dollars. Soros, George Soros took hundreds of millions
29 of dollars.
30
31 **WALLACE:** Mr. Trump --
32
33 **TRUMP:** --Let me just explain. All of her donors. Most of
34 her donors --

181

1

2 **WALLACE:** Mr. Trump --

3

4 **TRUMP:** Have done the same thing as I did. And you know
5 what she should have done? You know Hillary, what you
6 should have done? You should have changed the law when
7 you were a United States senator if you don't like it --

8

9 **WALLACE:** Thanks, we've heard this.

10

11 **TRUMP:** -- because your donors and special interests are
12 doing the same thing as I do except even more so. You
13 should have changed the law, but you won't change the
14 law because you take in so much money. I sat in my
15 apartment today on a very beautiful hotel down the
16 street.

17

18 **CLINTON:** Made with Chinese steel.

19

20 **TRUMP:** I will tell you I sat there. I sat there watching ad
21 after ad after ad, all false ads, all paid for by your friends
22 on Wall Street that gave so much money because they
23 know you're going to protect them. And frankly, you
24 should have changed the laws. If you don't like what I did,
25 you should have changed the laws.

26

27 **WALLACE:** Mr. Trump, I want to ask you about one last
28 question in this topic. You've been warning at rallies
29 recently that this election is rigged and that Hillary Clinton
30 is in the process of trying to steal it from you. Your running
31 mate Governor Pence pledged on Sunday that he and you,
32 his words, will absolutely accept the result of this election.
33 Today your daughter Ivanka said the same thing. I want to
34 ask you here on the stage tonight, do you make the same

1 commitment that you'll absolutely accept the result of the
2 election.
3
4 **TRUMP:** I will look at it at the time. I'm not looking at
5 anything now, I'll look at it at the time. What I've seen,
6 what I've seen, is so bad. First of all, the media is so
7 dishonest and so corrupt and the pile on is so amazing.
8 "The New York Times" actually wrote an article about it,
9 but they don't even care. It is so dishonest, and they have
10 poisoned the minds of the voters. But unfortunately for
11 them, I think the voters are seeing through it. I think
12 they're going to see through it, we'll find out on November
13 8th, but I think they're going to see through it. If you look -
14 -
15
16 **WALLACE:** But, but --
17
18 **TRUMP:** Excuse me, Chris. If you look at your voter rolls,
19 you will see millions of people that are registered to vote.
20 Millions. This isn't coming from me. This is coming from
21 Pew report and other places. Millions of people that are
22 registered to vote that shouldn't be registered to vote. So
23 let me just give you one other thing. I talk about the
24 corrupt media. I talk about the millions of people. I'll tell
25 you one other thing. She shouldn't be allowed to run. It's --
26 She's guilty of a very, very serious crime. She should not be
27 allowed to run, and just in that respect I say it's rigged
28 because she should never --
29
30 **WALLACE:** But, but --
31
32 **TRUMP:** Chris. She should never have been allowed to run
33 for the presidency based on what she did with e-mails and
34 so many other things.

183

1
2 **WALLACE:** But, sir, there is a tradition in this country, in
3 fact, one of the prides of this country is the peaceful
4 transition of power and no matter how hard fought a
5 campaign is that at the end of the campaign, that the loser
6 concedes to the winner. Not saying you're necessarily
7 going to be the loser or the winner, but that the loser
8 concedes to the winner and the country comes together in
9 part for the good of the country. Are you saying you're not
10 prepared now to commit to that principle?
11
12 **TRUMP:** What I'm saying is that I will tell you at the time.
13 I'll keep you in suspense, okay?
14
15 **CLINTON:** Well Chris, let me respond to that because
16 that's horrifying. You know, every time Donald thinks
17 things aren't going in his direction, he claims whatever it
18 is, is rigged against him. The FBI conducted a yearlong
19 investigation into my e-mails. They concluded there was
20 no case. He said the FBI was rigged. He lost the Iowa
21 caucus, he lost the Wisconsin primary, he said the
22 Republican primary was rigged against him. Then, Trump
23 University gets sued for fraud and racketeering. He claims
24 the court system and the federal judge is rigged against
25 him. There was even a time when he didn't get an Emmy
26 for his TV program three years in a row and he started
27 tweeting that the Emmys were rigged against him.
28
29 **TRUMP:** Should have gotten it.
30
31 (Laughter)
32
33 **CLINTON:** This is a mind-set. This is how Donald thinks,
34 and it's funny, but it's also really troubling. That is not the

1 way our democracy works. We've been around for 240
2 years. We've had free and fair elections. We've accepted
3 the outcomes when we may not have liked them, and that
4 is what must be expected of anyone standing on a debate
5 stage during a general election. You know, President
6 Obama said the other day when you're whining before the
7 game is even finished--
8
9   **(APPLAUSE)**
10
11 **WALLACE:** Hold on, folks.
12
13 **CLINTON:**-- It just shows you're not up to doing the job.
14 And let's be clear about what he's saying and what that
15 means. He's denigrating, he is talking down our
16 democracy. And I, for one, am appalled that somebody
17 who is the nominee of one of our two major parties would
18 take that kind of position.
19
20 **TRUMP:** I think what the FBI did and what the Department
21 of Justice did, including meeting with her husband, the
22 Attorney General, in the back of an airplane on the tarmac
23 in Arizona, I think it's disgraceful. I think it's a disgrace.
24
25 **WALLACE:** All right.
26
27 **TRUMP:** I think we've never had a situation so bad
28
29   **(APPLAUSE)**
30
31 **WALLACE:** Hold on, folks. This doesn't do any good for
32 anyone. Let's please continue the debate and let's move
33 onto the subject of foreign hotspots. The Iraqi offensive to
34 take back Mosul has begun. If they are successful in

1 pushing ISIS out of that city and out of all of Iraq, the
2 question then becomes, what happens the day after and
3 that's something whoever of you ends up as president is
4 going to have to confront. Will you put U.S. troops into
5 that vacuum to make sure ISIS doesn't come back or isn't
6 replaced by something even worse? Secretary Clinton, you
7 go first in this segment. You have two minutes.
8
9 **CLINTON:** Well, I am encouraged there is an effort led by
10 the Iraqi Army, supported by Kurdish forces and also given
11 the help and advice from the number of special forces and
12 other Americans on the ground, but I will not support
13 putting American soldiers into Iraq as an occupying force. I
14 don't think that is in our interest, and I don't think that
15 would be smart to do. In fact, Chris, I think that would be a
16 big red flag waving for ISIS to reconstitute itself. The goal
17 here is to take back Mosul. It's going to be a hard fight. I've
18 got no illusions about that. And then continue to press into
19 Syria to begin to take back and move on Raqqa, which is
20 the ISIS headquarters. I am hopeful that the hard work
21 that American military advisers have done will pay off and
22 that we will see a really successful military operation. But
23 we know we've got lots of work to do. Syria will remain a
24 hotbed of terrorism as long as the civil war aided and
25 abetted by the Iranians and the Russians continue, so I
26 have said, look, we need to keep our eye on ISIS. That's
27 why I want to have an intelligence surge that protects us
28 here at home, why we have to go after them from the air,
29 on the ground, online, why we have to make sure here at
30 home we don't let terrorists buy weapons. If you're too
31 dangerous to fly, you're too dangerous to buy a gun. And
32 I'm going to continue to push for a no-fly zone and safe
33 havens within Syria, not only to help protect the Syrians
34 and prevent the constant outflow of refugees, but to

1 frankly gain some leverage on both the Syrian government
2 and the Russians so that perhaps we can have the kind of
3 serious negotiation necessary to bring the conflict to an
4 end and go forward on a political track.
5

6 **WALLACE:** Mr. Trump, same question. If we are able to
7 push ISIS out of Mosul and out of Iraq, would you be
8 willing to put U.S. troops in there to prevent their return
9 or something else?
10

11 **TRUMP:** Let me tell you, Mosul is so sad. We had Mosul.
12 But when she left, she took everybody out, we lost Mosul.
13 Now we're fighting again to get Mosul. The problem with
14 Mosul and what they wanted to do is they wanted to get
15 the leaders of ISIS who they felt were in Mosul. About
16 three months ago, I started reading they want to get the
17 leaders and they're going to attack Mosul. Whatever
18 happened to the element of surprise, okay? We announce
19 we're going after Mosul. I've been reading about going
20 after Mosul now for about how long is it, Hillary, three
21 months? These people have all left. They've all left. The
22 element of surprise. Douglas MacArthur, George Patton
23 spinning in their graves at the stupidity of our country.
24

25 So we're now fighting for Mosul. That we had. All she had
26 to do was stay there, now we're going in to get it. But you
27 know who the big winner in Mosul is going to be after we
28 eventually get it -- and the only reason they did it is
29 because she's running for office of president and they
30 want to look tough. They want to look good. He violated
31 the red line in the sand, and he made so many mistakes.
32 He made all mistakes. That's why we have the great
33 Migration, but she wanted to look good for the election.
34 So they're going in.

1

2 But who is going to get Mosul really? We'll take Mosul
3 eventually. By the way, if you look at what's happening,
4 much tougher than they thought. Much, much tougher.
5 Much more dangerous, going to be more deaths than they
6 thought. But the leaders that we wanted to get are all
7 gone because they're smart. They say what do we need
8 this for. So Mosul is going to be a wonderful thing, and
9 Iran should write us a letter of thank you. Just like the
10 really stupid, the stupidest deal of all time, a deal that's
11 going to give Iran absolutely nuclear weapons. Iran should
12 write us yet another letter saying thank you very much
13 because Iran, as I said many years ago, Iran is taking over
14 Iraq. Something they've wanted to do forever, but we've
15 made it so easy for them. So we're now going to take
16 Mosul and you know who is going to be the beneficiary?
17 Iran. Boy are they making, they are outsmarting... Look
18 you're not there. You might be involved in that decision,
19 but you were there when you took everybody out of
20 Mosul and out of Iraq. You shouldn't have been in Iraq, but
21 you did vote for it. You shouldn't have been in Iraq, but
22 once you were in Iraq, you should have never left the way
23 -- the point is the big winner is going to be Iran.
24

25 **CLINTON:** Well, you know, once again Donald is implying
26 that he didn't support the invasion of Iraq. I said it was a
27 mistake. I said that years ago. He has consistently denied
28 what is --
29

30 **TRUMP:** Wrong.
31

32 **CLINTON:** -- is a very clear fact that before the invasion
33

34 **TRUMP:** Wrong.

1
2 **CLINTON:** -- he supported it. I just want everybody to go
3 google it. "Google Donald Trump Iraq" and you'll see the
4 dozens of sources which verify that he was for the invasion
5 of Iraq.
6
7 **TRUMP:** Wrong.
8
9 **CLINTON:** And you can hear the audio of him saying that.
10 Why does that matter? Well, it matters because he has not
11 told the truth about that position. I guess he believes it
12 makes him look better to contrast with me because I did
13 vote for it. But what's really important here is to
14 understand all the interplay. Mosul is a Sunni city. Mosul is
15 on the border of Syria, and yes, we do need to go after
16 Baghdadi, just like we went after Bin Laden while you were
17 doing "Celebrity apprentice" and we brought him to
18 justice. We need to go after the leadership, but we need
19 to get rid of them, get rid of their fighters. There are
20 several thousand fighters in Mosul. They've been digging
21 underground. They've been prepared to defend. It's going
22 to be tough fighting, but I think we can take back Mosul
23 and then we can move on into Syria and take back Raqqa.
24
25 This is what we have to do. I'm just am amazed that he
26 seems to think the Iraqi government and our allies and
27 everybody else launched the attack on Mosul to help me
28 in this election, but that's how Donald thinks, you know,
29 he always is looking for some conspiracy--
30
31 **TRUMP:** We don't gain anything. Iran is taking over --
32 **WALLACE:** Secretary Clinton --
33
34 **TRUMP:** Iran is taking over Iraq.

1

2 **CLINTON:** --his conspiracy theories-

3

4 **WALLACE:** Secretary Clinton --

5

6 **TRUMP:** We would have gained --

7

8 **CLINTON:** For quite sometime --

9

10 **WALLACE:** Secretary Clinton, it's an open discussion.
11 Secretary, please let Mr. Trump speak. Go ahead.

12

13 **CLINTON:** He's unfit. He proves it every time.

14

15 **TRUMP:** No, you're the one that's unfit. You know,
16 Wikileaks just actually came out. John Podesta said some
17 horrible things about you, and boy was he right. He said
18 some beauties. And you know Bernie Sanders, he said you
19 have bad judgment. You do. And if you think going into
20 Mosul after we let the world know we're going in and all of
21 the people we really wanted, the leaders are all gone, if
22 you think that was good, then you do. Now John Podesta
23 said you have terrible instincts. Bernie Sanders said you
24 have bad judgment. I agree with both.

25

26 **CLINTON:** Well you should ask Bernie Sanders who he is
27 supporting for President.

28

29 **TRUMP:** Which is a big mistake

30

31 **CLINTON:** And he said you are the most dangerous person
32 to run for president in the modern history of America. I
33 think he's right.

34

190

1 **WALLACE:** Let's turn to Aleppo. Mr. Trump, in the last
2 debate you were both asked about the situation in the
3 Syrian city of Aleppo, and I want to follow up on that
4 because you said several things in that debate which were
5 not true, sir. You said that Aleppo has basically fallen. In
6 fact, there are --
7
8 **TRUMP:** It's a catastrophe.
9
10 **WALLACE:** It is a catastrophe.
11
12 **TRUMP:** It's a mess. Have you seen it? Have you seen it?
13 Have you seen what's happened to Aleppo?
14
15 **WALLACE:** Sir, if I may finish my question.
16
17 **TRUMP:** Okay, so it hasn't fallen.Take a look at it.
18
19 **WALLACE:** Well there are quarter of a million people still
20 living there and being slaughtered.
21
22 **TRUMP:** That's right. And they are being slaughtered
23 because of bad decisions.
24
25 **WALLACE:** If I may just finish here. And you also said that
26 Syria and Russia are busy fighting ISIS. In fact, they have
27 been the ones who have been bombing and shelling
28 eastern Aleppo, and they just announced a humanitarian
29 pause, in effect admitting they have been bombing and
30 shelling in Aleppo. Would you like to clear that up, sir?
31
32 **TRUMP:** Well Aleppo is a disaster. It's a humanitarian
33 nightmare, but it has fallen from any standpoint. What do
34 you need, a signed document? Take a look at Aleppo. It is

1 so sad when you see what's happened. And a lot of this is
2 because of Hillary Clinton. Because what's happened is by
3 fighting Assad, who turned out to be a lot tougher than
4 she thought -- now she's going to say oh he loves Assad.
5 He's much tougher and much smarter than her and
6 Obama. And everyone thought he was gone two years
7 ago, three years ago. He aligned with Russia. He now also
8 aligned with Iran, who we made very powerful. We gave
9 them $150 billion back. We gave them $1.7 billion in cash.
10 I mean, cash, bundles of cash as big as this stage. We gave
11 them $1.7 billion.
12
13 Now they have lined -- he has aligned with Russia and with
14 Iran. They don't want ISIS, but they have other things
15 because we're backing, we're backing rebels. We don't
16 know who the rebels are. We're giving them lots of
17 money, lots of everything. We don't know who the rebels
18 are, and when and if -- and it's not going to happen
19 because you have Russia and you have Iran now. But if
20 they ever did overthrow Assad, you might end up with as
21 bad as Assad is. And he's a bad guy. But you may very well
22 end up with worse than Assad. If she did nothing, we
23 would be in much better shape. And this is what's caused
24 the Great Migration where she's taking in tens of
25 thousands of Syrian refugees, who probably in many cases
26 -- not probably, who are definitely in many cases, ISIS-
27 aligned. And we now have them in our country. Wait til
28 you see -- this is going to be the great Trojan horse. Wait
29 til you see what happens in the coming years. Lots of luck,
30 Hillary. Thanks a lot for doing a great job.
31
32 **WALLACE:** Secretary Clinton, you have talked about in the
33 last debate and again today that you would impose a no-
34 fly zone to try to protect the people of Aleppo and to stop

1 the killing there. President Obama has refused to do that
2 because he fears it's gonna draw us closer and deeper into
3 the conflict. And General Joseph Dunford, the Chairman of
4 the Joint Chiefs of Staff, says you want to impose a no-fly
5 zone, chances are you are going to get into a war, his
6 words, with Syria and Russia. So the question I have is first,
7 how do you respond to their concerns? Secondly, if you
8 impose a no-fly zone and a Russian plane violates that,
9 does President Clinton shoot that plane down?
10
11 **CLINTON:** Well Chris, first of all, I think a no-fly zone could
12 save lives and hasten the end of the conflict. I am well
13 aware of the really legitimate concerns you have
14 expressed from both the president and the general. This
15 would not be done just on the first day. This would take a
16 lot of negotiation and it would also take making it clear to
17 the Russians and the Syrians that our purpose is to provide
18 safe zones on the ground. We've had millions of people
19 leave Syria, and those millions of people inside Syria
20 who've been dislocated. So I think we could strike a deal
21 and make it very clear to the Russians and Syrians that this
22 was something that we believe the best interests of the
23 people on the ground in Syria. It would help us in the fight
24 against ISIS.
25
26 But I want to respond to what Donald said about refugees,
27 made these claims repeatedly. I am not going to let
28 anyone into this country who is not vetted, who we do not
29 have confidence in, but I am not going to slam the door on
30 women and children. That picture of that little 4-year-old
31 boy in Aleppo with the blood coming down his face while
32 he sat in an ambulance is haunting, and so we are going to
33 do very careful, thorough vetting. That does not solve our
34 internal challenges with ISIS and our need to stop

1 radicalization to work with American Muslim communities
2 who are on the front lines to identify and prevent attacks.
3 In fact, the killer of the dozens of people at the nightclub
4 in Orlando, the Pulse Night Club, was born in Queens, the
5 same place Donald was born. So let's be clear about what
6 the threat is and how we are best going to be able to meet
7 it. Yes, some of that threat emanates from over in Syria
8 and Iraq, and we've got to keep fighting. And I will defeat
9 ISIS. And some of it is we have to up our game and be
10 much smarter here at home.
11
12 **WALLACE:** Folks, I want to get into our final segment.
13
14 **TRUMP:** But I just have too... It's so ridiculous what she...
15 she will defeat ISIS. We should never have let ISIS happen
16 in the first place. And right now they are in 32 countries --
17
18 **WALLACE:** Mr. Trump --
19
20 **TRUMP:** Wait one second. They had a cease-fire three
21 weeks ago. A ceasefire: United States, Russia, Syria. And
22 during the cease-fire, Russia took over vast swathes of
23 land and then they said we don't want the cease-fire
24 anymore. We are so outplayed on missiles, on ceasefires.
25 They are outplayed. She wasn't there. I assume she had
26 nothing to do with it, but our country is so outplayed by
27 Putin and Assad and, by the way, and by Iran. Nobody can
28 believe how stupid our leadership is.
29
30 **WALLACE:** Mr. Trump, Secretary Clinton, no. We need to
31 move on to our final segment, and that is the national
32 debt, which has not been discussed until tonight. Our
33 national debt as a share of the economy, our GDP is now
34 77%. That's the highest since just after World War II, but

1 the non-partisan Committee for a Responsible Federal
2 Budget says, Secretary Clinton, under your plan, debt
3 would rise to 86% of GDP for the next ten years. Mr.
4 Trump, under your plan, they say it would rise to 105% of
5 GDP over the next ten years. The question is why are both
6 of you ignoring this problem? Mr. Trump, you go first.
7
8 **TRUMP:** Well I saw they're wrong because I'm going to
9 create tremendous jobs. And we're bringing GDP from
10 really 1%, which is what it is now, and if she got in, it
11 would be less than zero, but we're bringing it from 1% up
12 to 4%, and I actually think we can go higher than 4%. I
13 think you can go to 5% or 6%. And if we do, you don't have
14 to bother asking your question. Because we have a
15 tremendous machine. We will have created a tremendous
16 economic machine once again. To do that, we're taking
17 back jobs. We're not going to let our companies be raided
18 by other countries where we lose all our jobs. We don't
19 make our product anymore. It's very sad, but I am going to
20 create a... the kind of a country that we were from the
21 standpoint of industry. We used to be there. We've given
22 it up. We've become very, very sloppy. We've had people
23 that are political hacks making the biggest deals in the
24 world. Bigger than companies. You take these big
25 companies.
26
27 These trade deals are far bigger than these companies,
28 and yet we don't use our great leaders, many of whom
29 back me and many of whom backed Hillary, I must say, but
30 we don't use those people. Those are the people...these
31 are the greatest negotiators in the world. We have the
32 greatest business people in the world. We have to use
33 them to negotiate our trade deals. We use political hacks.
34 We use people that get the position because they made a

1 campaign contribution, and they're dealing with China and
2 people that are very much smarter than they are, so we
3 have to use our great people. But that being said, we will
4 create an economic machine the likes of which we haven't
5 seen in many decades and people, Chris, will again go back
6 to work, and they'll make a lot of money, and we'll have
7 companies that will ...will grow and expand and start from
8 new.
9
10 **WALLACE:** Secretary Clinton?
11
12 **CLINTON:** Well, first when I hear Donald talk like that and
13 know that his slogan is "Make America Great Again." I
14 wonder when he thought America was great. And before
15 he rushes and says, you know, before you and President
16 Obama were there, I think it's important to recognize that
17 he has been criticizing our government for decades. You
18 know, back in 1987, he took out an $100,000 ad in the
19 New York Times during the time when President Reagan
20 was president and basically said exactly what he just said
21 right now. That we were the laughing stock of the world.
22 He was criticizing President Reagan. This is the way Donald
23 thinks about himself, puts himself into, you know, the
24 middle and says, you know, 'I alone can fix it,' as he said
25 on the convention stage.
26
27 But if you look at the debt, which is the issue you asked
28 about, Chris, I pay for everything I'm proposing. I do not
29 add a penny to the national debt. I take that very seriously
30 because I do think it's one of the issues we've got to come
31 to grips with. So when I talk about how we're going to pay
32 for education, how we're going to invest in infrastructure,
33 how we're going to get the cost of prescription drugs
34 down, and a lot of the other issues that people talk to me

1 about all the time, I've made it very clear, we are going
2 where the money is. We are going to ask the wealthy and
3 corporations to pay their fair share. And there is no
4 evidence whatsoever that that will slow down or diminish
5 our growth. In fact, I think just the opposite. We'll have
6 what economists call middle outgrowth. We've got to get
7 back to rebuilding the middle class. The families of
8 America. That's where growth will come from. That's why I
9 want to invest in you. I want to invest in your family. And I
10 think that's the smartest way to grow the economy, to
11 make the economy fairer. And we just have a big
12 disagreement about this. It may be because of our
13 experiences. You know he started off with his dad as a
14 millionaire. I started off with my dad as a small
15 businessman.
16
17 **TRUMP:** We've heard this before, Hillary. We've heard this
18 before.
19
20 **CLINTON:** I think it's a difference that affects how we see
21 the world and what we want to do with the economy.
22
23 **WALLACE:** Time.
24
25 **TRUMP:** Thank you, Hillary. Could I just respond?
26
27 **WALLACE:** Well, no. Because we're running out of time.
28
29 **TRUMP:** Because I disagreed with Ronald Reagan very
30 strongly on trade. I disagreed with him. We should have
31 been much tougher on trade even then. I've been waiting
32 for years. Nobody does it right. And frankly now we're
33 going to do it right.
34

1   **WALLACE:** The one last area I want to get into with you in
2   the debate is the fact that the biggest driver of our debt is
3   entitlements, which is 60% of all federal spending. Now
4   the committee for a Responsible Federal Budget has
5   looked at both of your plans and they say neither of you
6   has a serious plan that is going to solve the fact that
7   Medicare is going to run out of money in the 2020s, Social
8   Security is going to run out of money in the 2030s, and at
9   that time, recipients are going to take huge cuts in their
10 benefits. In fact, the final question I want to ask you in this
11 regard is -- and let me start with you, Mr. Trump. Would
12 President Trump make a deal to save Medicare and Social
13 Security that included both tax increases and benefit cuts,
14 in effect a grand bargain on entitlements?
15
16 **TRUMP:** I'm cutting taxes. We're going to grow the
17 economy. It's going to grow in a record rate.
18
19 **WALLACE:** That's not going to help with entitlements.
20
21 **TRUMP:** It is going to totally help you. And one thing we
22 have to do is repeal and replace the disaster known as
23 Obamacare. It's destroying our country. It's destroying our
24 businesses, our small business and our big businesses. We
25 have to repeal and replace Obamacare. You take a look at
26 the kind of numbers that that will cost us in the year
27 [2017]. It is a disaster if we don't repeal and replace. It is
28 probably going to die of its own weight, but Obamacare
29 has to go. The premiums are going up 60%, 70%, 80%.
30 Next year, they're going to go up over 100%. And I'm really
31 glad that the premiums have started, at least the people
32 see what's happening because she wants to keep
33 Obamacare and she wants to make it even worse and it

1 can't get any worse. Bad health care at the most expensive
2 price. We have to repeal and replace Obamacare.
3
4 **WALLACE:** Secretary Clinton, same question because at
5 this point Social Security and Medicare are going to run
6 out -- the trust funds are going to run out of money. Will
7 you, as president, consider a grand bargain, a deal that
8 includes both tax increases and benefit cuts to try to save
9 both programs?
10
11 **CLINTON:** Well, Chris, I am record as saying we need to put
12 more money into Social Security Trust fund. That's part of
13 my commitment to raise taxes on the wealthy. My Social
14 Security payroll contribution will go up as will Donald's
15 assuming he can't figure out how to get out of it, but what
16 we want to do is --
17
18 **TRUMP:** Such a nasty woman.
19
20 **CLINTON:** Replenish the trust fund by making sure that we
21 have sufficient resources, and that will come from either
22 raising the cap and/or finding other ways to get more
23 money into it. I will not cut benefits. I want to enhance
24 benefits for low-income workers and for women who have
25 been disadvantaged by the current Social Security system.
26 But what Donald is proposing with these massive tax cuts
27 will result in a $20 trillion additional national debt. That
28 will have dire consequences for Social Security and
29 Medicare. And I'll say something about the Affordable
30 Care Act, which he wants to repeal. The affordable care
31 act extended the solvency of the Medicare trust fund. If he
32 repeals it, our Medicare problem gets worse.
33
34 **TRUMP:** Your husband disagrees with you.

1

2 **CLINTON:** We've got to go after the long-term health care
3 drivers. We've got to get costs down, increase value,
4 emphasize wellness. I have a plan for doing that, and I
5 think that we will be able to get entitlement spending
6 under control but with more resources and smart
7 decisions.

8

9 **WALLACE:** This is a final time, probably to both of your
10 delight, that you're going to be on the stage together in
11 this campaign. I would like to end it on a positive note. You
12 had not agreed to closing statements, but it seems to me
13 in a funny way that might make it more interesting
14 because you haven't prepared closing statements. So I
15 would for each of you to take -- and we're going to put a
16 clock up -- a minute as the final question, in the final
17 debate, to tell the American people why they should elect
18 you to be the next president. This is another new mini
19 segment. Secretary Clinton, it's your turn to go first.

20

21 **CLINTON:** Well I would like to say to everyone watching
22 tonight that I'm reaching out to all Americans, Democrats,
23 Republicans and independents, because we need
24 everybody to help make our country what it should be, to
25 grow the economy, to make it fairer, to make it work for
26 everyone. We need your talents, your skills, your
27 commitment, your energy, your ambition. You know, I've
28 been privileged to see the presidency up close, and I know
29 the awesome responsibility of protecting our country and
30 the incredible opportunity of working to try to make life
31 better for all of you. I have made the cause of children and
32 families really my life's work. That's what my mission will
33 be in the presidency. I will stand up for families against
34 powerful interests, against corporations. I will do

1 everything that I can to make sure that you have good jobs
2 with rising incomes, that your kids have good educations
3 from preschool through college. I hope you will give me a
4 chance to serve as your president.
5
6 **WALLACE:** Secretary Clinton, thank you. Mr. Trump?
7
8 **TRUMP:** She's raising the money from the people she
9 wants to control. Doesn't work that way. But when I
10 started this campaign, I started it very strongly. It's called
11 Make America Great Again. We're going to make America
12 great. We have a depleted military. It has to be helped. It
13 has to be fixed. We have the greatest people on Earth in
14 our military. We don't take care of our veterans. We take
15 care of illegal immigrants, people that come into our
16 country illegally better than we take care of our vets. That
17 can't happen. Our policemen and women are
18 disrespected. We need law and order, but we need justice
19 too. Our inner cities are a disaster. You get shot walking to
20 the store. They have no education. They have no jobs. I
21 will do more for African-Americans and Latinos that she
22 can do for ten lifetimes. All she's done is talk to the
23 African-Americans and to the Latinos, but they get the
24 vote and then they come back, they say 'we'll see you in
25 four years.' We are going to make America strong again
26 and we are going to make America great again and it has
27 to start now. We cannot take four more years of Barack
28 Obama, and that's what you get when you get her.
29
30 **WALLACE:** Thank you both. Secretary Clinton –
31
32   **[Applause]**
33

1 Hold on just a moment, folks. I want to thank you both for
2 participating in all three of these debates. That brings us to
3 the end of the three debates sponsored by the
4 Commission of Presidential Debates. We want to thank the
5 university of Nevada Las Vegas and its students for having
6 us. Now the decision is up to you. While millions have
7 already voted, election day, November 8, is just 20 days
8 away. One thing everyone here can agree on is we hope
9 you will go vote. It is one of the honors and obligations of
10 living in this great country. Thank you and good night.
11
12   **[Applause]**
13
14